HAPPILY EVER AFTER
(AND OTHER MYTHS ABOUT DIVORCE)

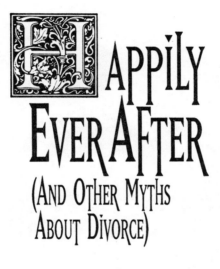

Happily Ever After

(And Other Myths About Divorce)

Ron Durham

VICTOR BOOKS

A DIVISION OF SCRIPTURE PRESS PUBLICATIONS INC.
USA CANADA ENGLAND

All Scripture quotations, unless otherwise indicated, are taken from the *Holy Bible, New International Version*®. Copyright © 1973, 1978, 1984 by International Bible Society. Used by permission of Zondervan Publishing House. All rights reserved. Quotations marked KJV are from the *Authorized (King James) Version.*

Copyediting: Afton Rorvik
Cover Design: Scott Rattray
Cover Photo: Manuel S. Morales

Library of Congress Cataloging-in-Publication Data

Durham, Ron.
    Happily ever after / by Ron Durham.
      p.   cm.
    Includes bibliographical references.
    ISBN 1-56476-069-3
    1. Divorce—United States. 2. Marriage—United States.
  I. Title.
  HQ834.D87 1992   92-21506
  306.89—dc20   CIP

1 2 3 4 5 6 7 8 9 10 Printing/Year 97 96 95 94 93

CONTENTS

INTRODUCTION

aye and I found the Bahama Islands a perfect place for a honeymoon, as many other lovers have discovered. We sunbathed on the sparkling beaches and swam in the crystalline Caribbean. We caught a ride on a small sailboat skippered by a grizzled native and gasped at the breathtaking underwater scenes which appeared in a window box he thrust just under the water's surface. We ate the sweet meat of the shellfish that has made the huge, pink conch shells famous, dutifully learning to pronounce it "conk." We bought native jewelry, read while it rained, and generally made happy tourists of ourselves.

Only one thing kept it all from being a fairly typical Caribbean honeymoon. Faye and I were not celebrating a wedding but the failure of our anticipated divorce.

Although I am a minister with training and experience in saving marriages, I fully expected to add ours to the 1.2 million others that failed that year (the figure is higher now). After years of struggle and several separations, I had exhausted my ability to deal with our fundamental differences over finances, raising children, lifestyles, and religion. Personality differences that had once seemed of little consequence had mushroomed until we both felt the force

7

of the classic phrase, "You're not the person I married."
How familiar we were with that old line, "The feeling is
gone." I took a job in another town. Both of us learned
that if we had to, we could survive apart from each other.
With such a long list of differences and difficulties, divorce
seemed inevitable.

Yet, there we were in the Bahamas, celebrating the fact
that our attempt at dissolution just didn't work.

While a great deal is written about why *marriages* fail,
we hear less about the fact that *divorces* aren't always a
huge success either. Our story and the others recorded in
this book supply testimony that is too often ignored in the
court of public opinion. Until recently, conventional wisdom held that the emotional pain of such drastic differences as we experienced is best treated by divorce. Now,
at last, even secular marriage counselors are acknowledg-
ing that the negative effects of divorce are much greater
than was thought.

"We used to focus more on personal growth," admits
one experienced marriage counselor. "If personal growth
meant you had to get a divorce, that was a valid conclusion." Now, she says, experts are recognizing that divorce
"has not been a particularly good answer for marital problems."[1] Says another counselor: "I originally thought that
staying together in turmoil was more traumatic than making the break, that striking down the taboos about divorce
was part of modern enlightenment. I was wrong."[2]

This book tells the real-life stories of those who have
caused these therapists and many others to change their
minds. It cites the experience of those who say, with thirty-
one-year-old Billie L., "I thought divorce was the answer
to all my problems. The reality was that it was only the
beginning."

In the pages that follow you will meet people who:

- found that while divorce dissolved their marriage, it
  did not resolve their problems;
- tried divorce as a cure for their marital ills, only to

find that the remedy was worse than the disease;
- discovered that they were wrong when they thought that "nothing could be worse than living together like this";
- found that the needs they thought were not being met in their marriage were nothing compared to the needs created by divorce.

America has become a litigious society in the area of marriage as much as in the area of personal injury and other damages. Marital offenses abuse our rights, and the natural reaction is to redress such wrongs with a lawsuit. Divorce is so much a part of the air we breathe that we fail to notice some people are choking on it.

In sounding this smog alert, I do not deny that some marriages cannot and should not be sustained. Especially in cases of abuse, divorce may well be the kind of radical surgery necessary to save a life. Neither do I pretend that there can be no life after divorce—even one that was a tragic mistake.

But I do protest the colossal fallacy of assuming that because divorce is sometimes necessary, it is *usually* the best route toward escaping unhappiness. The fact is, with the permissiveness of the 1960s, divorce assumed a positive reputation that is out of all proportion with the blunt negatives experienced by many who try it. It is a step taken with the culturally supported belief that it enhances life, when in fact, it often impoverishes it.

This book does not seek to heap guilt on those who find it necessary to divorce, or to harp on the fact that God said, "I hate divorce" (Mal. 2:16). It simply offers evidence from the laboratory of life—many *people* who have tried it hate divorce.

You will appreciate the courage of the witnesses assembled here. They are to be thanked for being willing to make themselves so vulnerable in the hope that they could help someone else avoid the trauma they have experienced. They have dared to recall painful experiences they would rather forget, and they have retraced footsteps they wish they had not taken.

At one point in compiling this book, I worried that it would be too negative. In reality, the book contains happy endings and happy beginning-agains, as in our own Bahamian honeymoon. Besides, some of the most positive results are obtained by negatives. It is a positive thing when someone cries out, "Take shelter!" in the face of a rampaging storm. As healthy as a positive mental attitude may be for surviving both a divorce and a dismal marriage, we dare not paste an artificial happy face over the fact that this year some 3 million people—many of them innocent children—will be ravaged and uprooted as divorce storms across the landscape of their lives.

Allow yourself to benefit from those who now wish they had summoned the strength to be more patient and understanding in their marriage, having learned that this effort would not have been as demanding as the effort they must make now to survive the divorce. Take seriously those who wish they had been more willing to forgive wrongs, or to compromise, or to be less selfish. Risk sharing the pain of those who say they did not anticipate how divorce would traumatize their children or reduce them to such desperate financial straits.

And if divorce is a possibility in your own life as you read this book, test your own capacity simply to wait. For here you will read of those who wish they had hung on, however grim the situation, until their spouse negotiated some difficult life passage, or until some briefly boiling body-mind chemical subsided, or until sheer time could heal an ill no other therapy could touch.

I sat with a group of divorced people discussing their regrets and sharing the kinds of stories you will read about in this book. At one point, Bill W. spoke up: "I've been noticing something as we've talked. I believe that if someone contemplating divorce sat in on this session, he would change his mind quickly."

You're invited simply to sit in, through the following

pages, on a session like the one described above.

Some of the people you will hear from had such miserable divorces that they remarried their ex-spouses. Of course this isn't possible—or even desirable—in many cases. Yet, if you are considering divorce, these stories may induce you to "remarry" (recommit to) your present spouse before tensions in your marriage become a chasm that cannot be bridged.

Now here are some friends I want you to meet.

PART I

Myths about Divorce

When a marriage runs into trouble, several half-truths often surface, explained by clichés such as, "Being alone would be better than fighting like this," or "She's draining the bank account as it is, so it wouldn't cost any more to live alone," or "Kids are resilient—they'll bounce back," or "If my husband were ever unfaithful, this marriage would have to end."

One by one, these half-truths turn out to be myths.

Myth 1
I'll be just fine by myself.

CHAPTER ONE

Alone at Last
(Where Did I Go Wrong?)

ill M. knew what she wanted, and it wasn't her husband Mack. He drank heavily, stayed out late, and was financially irresponsible. She recalls her feelings with the liberal use of the "perpendicular pronoun": *"I* decided *I* could not continue to live in that fashion, and *I* did not want *my* children brought up in that kind of environment. After all, *I* had made all of the concessions and given *my* all to the relationship. In fact, *I* was a modern, independent, self-sufficient woman who could take care of *myself* and *my* children. *I* then packed *my* 'tent' and children and told Mack to call me when he grew up."

The Blocking Effects of Pain

Jill was experiencing the fact that pain is by definition self-centered; the self is the only instrument we have that can truly register pain. Even if I am marvelously empathetic and hurt *for* someone else, *I* feel the pain. Jill's marital pain occupied all nerve paths, consumed all her emotional energy, and caused her to forget what did *not* hurt in the relationship. Pain blocked her capacity to project herself into the future and to remember such simple truths as the

15

fact that being alone can be painful too. Her pain enabled her to rationalize that "I couldn't feel any more alone than I feel in this marriage." It made her need for "space" the one overwhelming objective on her life agenda.

Only a few months after her divorce, Jill found herself in the "one less egg to fry" syndrome. She had plenty of space—so much that she rushed about frantically to fill it. She rushed to work, rushed home, always scurrying to stay ahead of the stark loneliness of single parenting during the mornings and evenings, and sleeping single at night. She prayed in vain for some way to turn back the time.

Pearl W.'s regrets are also poignantly related to being unable to project herself into a future without Bob, whom she divorced. "I miss the friendship and the closeness we had between us. We were a good team and worked well together." Dating only made matters worse, she says. "I realized that Bob had qualities and standards that are unique. Sometimes I feel that I will never meet another man that is as good as Bob."

Shirley Q. reflects on the loneliness she has felt since her divorce—loneliness she might have predicted had the pain of her marriage not kept her from projecting herself into a lonely future.

"I have always had a problem with being alone. I was very dependent on my husband in a lot of areas, especially socially. My social life revolved around him and his occupation (he was a minister). There were many social opportunities while we were married that I was sort of dropped from after our separation.

"I have not dealt with this well. I am lonely a lot. I find it hard to move into new crowds or situations. I have done very little dating. I find it hard to entertain alone. I don't really have a group of single friends. Somehow single women don't really seem to fit in with each other very well. I also find it hard to make new plans and to dream new dreams. I just plod along one day at a time."

A divorcé wrote advice columnist Ann Landers to share the pain of feeling shut out of the lives of the wife and family he left behind. "It hit me when I was a guest at our eldest son's wedding," he wrote. "That's all I was—a guest. I am no longer considered part of the family. . . . I miss my sons, especially around holiday time. I am going to try to build some bridges, but the prospects don't look very promising after being out of their lives for ten years."[1]

Corrine F. describes the pain of divorce in terms of an amputation. "It's like having a limb amputated," she says. "I understand that for a period of time it still feels like it's there. And I think a marriage can be like that. Even though it's over, it feels like something's still there. And it hurts."

Lonely or Codependent?

While the main aim of this book is to warn that many people have found divorce worse than marriage, I also acknowledged in the Introduction that some people *need* to divorce—particularly those who are being abused. Unfortunately, my research turned up a few people who were so lonely after divorce that they longed to go back into destructive relationships. They had difficulty distinguishing between positive love for the ex-spouse and unhealthy dependency upon him or her.

One woman moved out after her husband started drinking heavily, staying out late, and being financially irresponsible. Although he kept their house at first, his spending habits soon forced him to lose the house, his job, and his car. Unfortunately, pity or dependency overwhelmed her good sense, and she allowed him to move in with her—a decision she almost paid for with her life. He beat her unmercifully. She kicked him out, but he returned and shot her four times and was sent to prison.

Even after all this, she speaks wistfully of their relationship and blames herself for not trusting God to solve their problems instead of running away from them.

Of course such statements indicate the urgency of getting good counseling before and after divorcing—in sessions that probe not only the immediate symptoms of the breakdown of the marriage, but also areas of codependency and unhealthy "symbiosis"—defined here as the inability to grow and be healthy apart from a destructive relationship. Genuine love has regard not only for the spouse but also for one's self and for the relationship itself. These issues are so subjective that couples often need to discuss them before a third party in order to weigh the ability to live alone (and perhaps the necessity of it) against the cost of staying in the marriage.

One for the Price of Two

The failure to measure their capacity to get along without a mate is only a portion of the regret many divorced people experience. Single parents know a special kind of loneliness. They pay the price of two parents for the privilege of entering the fight to raise children adequately, but they have to fight by themselves.

Betsy was an abused wife. After years of being physically and emotionally battered, she finally fled the house at night with her three children while her husband was gone. It seemed the only alternative. Now, fifteen years later, she is still struggling to make ends meet. She is uneasy about her status at work because she is absent so much tending to the needs of the two children who are still in school. "If I had known what I know now," she says, "I would have found some way to get my husband into counseling, or just separated while he got help—anything would have been better than this."

Betsy's statement reminds us that being alone can have greater consequences than the psychic state of loneliness. Here are some specific problems single parents often face.

1. The inability to make decisions. Divorced men, for example, are often stymied when asked to help a teenage girl decide what high school courses to take. Single mothers may find it tough to decide on whether to repair the old car or sign a long-term note for a new one.

2. The feeling of being overwhelmed by responsibility. It is one thing to psych yourself up into believing you can tend to all the parenting details by yourself, but another to find yourself having to keep a business appointment on the very evening your daughter is in the sixth-grade play.

3. Feelings of guilt at having caused the children to lose a parent. One woman looked back on her divorce and lamented, "I regret not standing by him in his time of need. I regret cheating my children out of a father."

4. Not being able to be both mother and father. Again, it is easy to say that since a delinquent or irresponsible spouse wasn't around to do much parenting anyway, you can wear both hats. Many dads find it tough to introduce an adolescent daughter to the exciting world of makeup.

5. Conflicts between self-interest and children's interest. Parental *pairs* cover and substitute for each other endlessly—"I have an appointment at the hairdresser, so can you take Jimmy to his piano lesson?" But the process is so unconscious that it's hard to calculate whether you can handle (a) everything on your own, (b) knowing and asserting when your needs should take priority over the child's and (c) the guilt that often comes when you do so.

6. Feelings of financial inadequacy. This is especially true if one's previous lifestyle was maintained by two incomes.

David Lambert, a Christian editor, speaks of how all this works from a practical standpoint. "Single moms, especially if they have little boys, usually worry about discipline, and single dads usually worry that they're not being sufficiently gentle, understanding, and nurturing."[2] As bleak as this picture is, some divorced parents who have been relieved of their children by a court decree will tell you that not having such parenting problems brings its own pangs of loneliness.

Albert L., a twenty-eight-year-old security officer, describes it: "I have three children, all of whom live with

their mother over 300 miles away. I can't afford to see
them but a couple of times a year. It's like having your
insides torn out to have them kept just out of your reach
like that. I miss their big eyes on Christmas morning and
their late-night giggles."

When All Else Fails

We noted earlier that Betsy thinks a separation might have
been worth considering, given the tough times she's experienced living alone. When all other means of saving the
marriage have failed—and if both partners strictly avoid
other relationships—separations can help by enabling a
couple to test the loneliness factor.

Leon and Gloria W. were married for six and a half
years—long enough to realize how different they were.
The differences loomed so large they separated. Assuming
like so many others that separation is just the preliminary
to a permanent split, they divorced after a year.

But "our divorce simply failed," Leon says, primarily
because of the aching, empty void both he and his wife
found at the center of life without each other. "Through
the years we had established this emotional bond that was
just stronger than our differences. And the year's separation gave us time to reflect on what we had together."

Gloria started going to a single parent church fellowship
and invited the other single parent she knew best—her ex-
husband Leon. Soon they were remarried. "Things aren't
perfect," Leon is frank to admit. "One of the things I still
have to work on is acceptance of differences," he says.
"We came from very different backgrounds—social, economic, religious. Also, we were a blended family, and
there were problems with my being a stepparent. We
probably are more different in the area of parenting than
on issues just between the two of us." But for Leon and
Gloria all their differences put together weigh less than
the burden of loneliness when they were apart.

Myth 2
The financial strain of divorce can't compare
to the tension in this marriage.

CHAPTER TWO

The High Cost of Leaving

here is nothing like a divorce to prove that two people *can* live more cheaply than one. Countless marital partings that seem to "work" at first because they relieve immediate pain turn out to be disasters as bills pile up month after month.

Even at Best, It's Worse

Even when both spouses are trying to be fair, divorce is expensive. Meet Carl and Katie Adamson, a minister and his wife, whose story will be told in more detail in chapter 8. When the couple separated, Katie went to work for her father in California. She didn't count on the high cost of living there. Katie had far more support than many single parents—yet she could not have imagined the financial battle into which her new life plunged her.

"I had a college education," she says, "but I wasn't sure how much good it would do me since I'd been out of the work force for seven years. I was fortunate to have a family business to go to. I was paid $25,000 a year, and because it was a family business, if the kids were sick and I had to be away from work, I was covered. I had Grandma to baby-sit and aunts, and my sister helped. I was given extra mon-

21

ey and all, and I still wasn't making it.

Despite all this help from relatives, Katie paid about $1,000 a month in child care. "If I had been by myself, I don't know what would have happened. I was a good worker, I was working hard, I wasn't living extravagantly, my car was paid for—and I still wasn't making it."

Her husband Carl was struggling too. As a minister, he was fortunate to get suitable work in another field. Yet he says, "I couldn't support both of us on what I was making. I was paying over $800 a month in rent, and she was paying over $900. Our combined incomes brought in about $55,000 a year—that's not a bad income, and we still weren't making it. When we got back together, we were able to save about $3,000 in the first year."

As explained in chapter 8, the Adamsons didn't even have the expense of finalizing a divorce. Still, they ran up bills for the attorney's fees involved with the separation, the counseling, the moves, separate housing, and child care. "I figure the whole thing must have cost us something on the order of $12,000," Carl estimates.

Katie adds: "I just have this feeling in the pit of my stomach for the woman who doesn't have a decent job or a family to fall back on. The statistics show that single moms are getting closer and closer to the poverty level. Their income goes down drastically. It's an economic reality. Unless you're a high-powered businesswoman and can employ a nanny, you're just not going to make it on your own."

Feelings vs. Finances

Talking about money and divorce can seem to be missing the point. Isn't the pain *relational* or *emotional*, rather than economic? Indeed, some hurting people view such a discussion as materialistic or irrelevant. Their feelings tell them that the main issue at hand is to dissolve this painful relationship. To put the divorce decision on an economic basis can seem like bringing up the case for humane execution during an argument about capital punishment—the main point is whether the life (or the relationship) should be ended; why waste time talking about ways and means?

But many people who regret their divorces wish they could have treated the financial results as more central to their decision. Caught up in the trauma of a bad marriage, their scream, *"I want out!"* drowned out all thought about financial consequences: *"Anything* would be better than living like this! My sanity is worth more than all the money in the world!" Clinical psychologist Diane Medved has a wise response to such thinking:

> These are valid points, but your sanity and peace of mind can be completely destroyed if you find yourself in pressured or depressed financial circumstances. It's one thing to pontificate about how surroundings don't matter to you and how you can blithely scrounge a gourmet dinner out of trash bins, but it's another to have to actually do it night after night. . . .
>
> After a divorce you either feel more desperate or more dependent: more desperate if you must now rely on only yourself to try to maintain the standard of living you had or desire; more dependent if you must look to your ex-spouse for support.[1]

It's Not Women's Liberation

Women usually still suffer more than men from the economic effects of divorce. Ironically, recent attempts to make divorce laws more equitable and humane have actually worked against fair treatment. "No-fault" divorce, instituted in California in 1970, was intended to reduce the bitterness and acrimony of divorce by removing the necessity of placing blame for the marriage's failure. The new laws were also designed to recognize the equality of women and men before the law, instead of assuming that "the little woman" needed special treatment and protection.

With such good intentions, no-fault divorce swept the country.

Unfortunately, the no-fault laws in effect often discriminated against women. Researcher Lenore Weitzman found that in general the new laws had the unexpected effect of bringing "hardship, impoverishment and disillusionment for divorced women (and their children)."[2]

How did this happen? For one thing, if no one is found "at fault" in a court of law, it can be more difficult to place responsibility for child support. Under no-fault divorce laws, countless men who were relatively well-off were not held accountable for helping support their children. Often, a woman who had been "only a housewife" during her marriage was forced to enter, unprepared, into the job market to provide for her children, with little or no help from her husband. She may have had equal rights, but she did not have equal training.

A second inequity surfaced when no-fault laws split a couple's assets down the middle, 50-50. That sounds fair enough—until you consider that in many cases a couple's primary assets were skills, education, or experience that the man had acquired with the help of his wife. She often cared for the children and otherwise played a supportive role so her husband could get training and develop the professional or trade skills or the business acumen that resulted in their real assets. In effect, she helped her husband increase his own earning capacity at the expense of her own. It can be argued that the couple's most valuable asset is not their real property but the man's capacity to produce income—which is very hard to divide with his wife even though she helped him develop that capacity. So when the house and car and bank accounts are split 50-50, the woman again comes out the loser—especially in view of the fact that 90 percent of the time she is awarded primary custody of the children.

Comparing the income of divorced men and women with the needs of each, Weitzman discovered that, on the average, divorced *men* enjoy a *42 percent rise* in their standard of living in the first year after a divorce, while divorced *women* and their children must cope with a 73 *percent decline* in their standard of living[3] (emphasis mine).

The unfairness of the new, "fairer" laws has become a major impetus for legal reforms. A few states have already started *requiring* the divorce court to assess some degree of blame or responsibility in order to make more equitable decisions regarding finances and child custody.

But doesn't child support or alimony take up the slack? Hardly. A census bureau report said that as of the spring of 1988, 9.4 million single mothers were caring for their children on their own—out of an estimated _____ divorcées. (No one knows for sure just how many divorcées there are in the U.S.) The study showed that of the divorced mothers whose ex-spouses were supposed to help, only 70 percent receive the child support payments they are due.[4]

Lenore Weitzman's research turned up even more dismal figures, indicating that less than half of divorced fathers comply fully with court ordered child support. And it's not the lower income men who aren't paying. "Men who earn between $30,000 and $50,000 a year are just as likely to fail to pay child support as those who earn less than $20,000 a year," she reported.[5]

Men Suffer Too

Of course, men themselves can also be victims of the high cost of leaving. Gary Richmond, who directs the single parents ministry at First Evangelical Free Church in Fullerton, California, tells of advising a man whose wife had sued for divorce to give her his equity in a car that was worth $2,000.

"Isn't that like handing her a thousand dollars?" the man asked.

"Not really," Richmond said. "If you decide to fight for the car or your share of it, you will spend that much anyway." He went on to explain that many lawyers charge by the hour, at $125 to $140 an hour.

Unfortunately, the man wound up allowing such a lawyer to inflame his passions and try to get all he could out
of the divorce. His final cost was more than $7,000.[6]

And that was a "simple" divorce.

Minister and counselor Jim Talley has a formula for
bringing people considering divorce face-to-face with reality. "You think it's a simple matter of dividing your assets
by two?" he asks. And he answers, "That is seldom how it
works. In reality you add up all the assets and divide that
by four. When the divorce is final, she gets one-fourth, he
gets another fourth, and the two attorneys split the rest."[7]

More Than Money

Some divorced people discover that even when careful
calculation indicates they can squeak by on what they both
make, it's impossible to budget items such as work lost
because of emotional upset. When Dana F. found her husband with another woman, she went into shock. For hours
she couldn't stop crying, then finally cried herself to sleep.
The kids got themselves off to school, and Dana went out
by the pool and sat in a catatonic state for eight or nine
hours. She was simply disabled by it all. Soon she had
depleted all her savings and had to sell her small business
far under its market price because it took her so long to
regain her ability simply to work—much less cope otherwise.

This link between finances and the emotions goes much
deeper too. Author Deidre Laiken describes the effect of
her divorced parents' arguments over money. Now, when
she hears someone say that he or she intends to take the
estranged spouse for "everything I can get," she shudders
and wonders "if the rage I observed my divorcing parents
displace onto money matters will continue to prevent me
from giving everything I have to give."[8]

CHAPTER THREE

"For the Sake of the Children"

n the days before divorce came to be so much in vogue, many couples whose marriage was less than perfect toughed it out "for the sake of the kids." Sometime in the 1960s, this changed. In the age of personal fulfillment, it was more important to meet our own needs. To accommodate any vestiges of continued concern for the effect of divorce on children, we were told, "Kids are resilient and flexible. They'll get over it sooner than you think."

Now we discover that they get over it later than we thought, if they ever do. With the burgeoning necessity of support groups for "Adult Children of Divorced Parents," counselors are taking a second look at the impact of divorce on children.

Getting the Kids' Attention

At a recent retreat for 400 junior and senior high school students in California, participants gathered light-heartedly—and loudly—in the cafeteria to hear seminar leaders announce the topics available at the retreat. The first four speakers had a problem getting the students' attention. After all, it was a retreat, and time for fun.

Then the fourth speaker announced his topic: handling

home life when your parents are separated or divorced. He would deal with divided loyalties, when your mom and your dad have split and both want you on their side, getting along in blended families, and handling the guilt you feel about the divorce having been your fault. The fact that it was this offering that brought a sudden hush over the entire hall is a sad commentary on our times.

Sally, an eighteen-year-old, speaks frankly to an interviewer: "You never get over it; that's the thing. I mean people are real worried about you at first, but then they figure it's been a couple of years and you must be adjusted. . . . But it never goes away. It always is part of you, and it affects things you do."[1]

Never get over it? Author Deidre Laiken writes:

> My parents were divorced fifteen years ago. At my high school graduation, for the sake of appearances, they sat next to each other. That was the last time I ever saw them together. They have engaged in only the barest of conversations since that day. But often when I am alone I close my eyes and imagine them standing side by side. I justify the fantasy by saying, "I would just like to see them in the same room together. . . . " My fantasy reveals a primitive longing. I know I still feel the loss.[2]

This is not atypical. Some experts believe that "the interruption of a continuous relationship with a loving and nurturing parent invariably leaves scars that do not heal completely and may affect the child's future ability to form relationships and become a good parent."[3]

Even when it doesn't come to divorce, children bear a cruel share of any constant parental quarreling. Gary Richmond, the singles minister you met in the previous chapter, tells of the effect of marital strife on his five-year-old daughter, Julie. Hearing her sobbing after he and his wife had quarreled long and loud, he peeked into her room and asked what was wrong.

"Daddy," Julie said, "will you hold me?"

As he held her close, she said in a tremulous voice, "It's just that I don't know if anyone loves me anymore."[4]

Weighing the Leaving against the Pain

Carl Adamson, the minister you met in chapter 2, makes no apology for weighing the stress of staying together against the pain—for both parents and children—of leaving.

"I really question the wisdom of counsel that says not to stay together for the sake of the kids," he said. "I think that there are times when that's the only thing couples have, and I thank God for it. Not just for the stability it gives the kids, but it buys time for the couple.

"I can't tell you how painful it was to have to leave my kids, both initially and then at the end of visits. After a period of five or six weeks when I wasn't able to see our little one-year-old, she didn't recognize me. She didn't know who I was! The blank look on her face . . .

"And to leave my children after an extended weekend visit—the way they cried—it was like I was ripping their arms off or something. I would drive away crying and screaming. The frustration that built up was excruciating. I can understand now, someone kidnapping their kids."

Carl's wife Katie remembers it from the children's perspective. "The comments they made to both of us would just make us want to cry. One time Jody came home from Sunday School and said, 'Mom, Elizabeth is so, so lucky—her parents had got divorced, and they got together again!'

"Our middle child Jock was three when we separated, and his anger was incredible. And it was directed at me—which was really hard for me to deal with." It was the common situation of Dad being there only for a fun trip, while Mom got to take the brunt of the kids' reaction against everyday discipline.

"Jock's anger came out in kicking and hitting—just tantrums. And he couldn't express it verbally. I knew what was driving him crazy, but I couldn't help him put it into words. But the minute we got back together he was fine.

"Our oldest child, who was five, handled it beautifully, appearance-wise. She could articulate what upset her. She'd cry, and she could say what was bothering her — she understood it all, as much as a five-year-old can. But then after we were reconciled, the anxiety was just incredible. It was like, 'This is so neat I don't want to believe it, because it may not last.' And if we had any kind of disagreement or discussion, it would be really hard on her. It was a long time before she really felt secure."

Love-Hate Confusion

Some of the regrets of those I interviewed focused not on the divorce itself, but on how it was presented to the children involved. Jennifer S. divorced her husband of twenty-three years after he, in her view, "was responsible for the emotional ending of the marriage." In psychological terms, he was passive-aggressive, setting up roadblocks in the marriage and blaming Jennifer for not jumping over them. But since she was the one who filed for divorce, she was blamed by her grown children for the official breakup of the marriage.

Jennifer defended herself the only way she knew how — by angrily telling the children how she had been victimized. But she failed to calculate the deep confusion divorce can bring even to adult children. Her self-pity and anger set up the reverse effect every counselor has seen. "The children loved their father," Jennifer now sees, "and they weren't going to just listen to me and abandon him. I suppose they got tired of listening to me bellyache."

Finally, with the help of counseling, Jennifer was able to see that she was hurting herself most of all by remaining in the posture of a victim. "I think it's especially easy for women to move into being a victim," she says. "And I still haven't gotten rid of all the anger. It's probably why I haven't moved on. I haven't socialized or anything."

It's hard for a brutalized spouse to imagine that his or

her children could love a brute. The fact is, it often takes a great deal of brutality for children to actually hate a victimizing parent. The commandment "Honor thy father and thy mother" is not merely from a Jewish law book—it also seems to be included in our genetic code. The victimized spouse must remember that this code is embedded even in the cells of the child's eyes as he looks at the victimizing parent. For one of the damaging effects of divorce on children is that they wind up with confused feelings of both love and hate—often for both parents.

Elaine S. had good reason to divorce her husband. He had abused their children. In the well-known game of "Choose Sides," some family members and friends took her husband's side, telling Elaine's eldest daughter, "Your mother is tearing the family apart. She's stabbing your father in the back!" As an almost dutiful consequence, the daughter began having horrible nightmares of knives and blood and images of death—which persist to this writing, several years after the divorce.

Then things got worse. "I didn't realize the kind of person I would become as a single parent, with the additional stress," Elaine said. "My ex-husband died not long after the divorce, and I had to cope with that. I just kind of shut down emotionally and wasn't available to my children even when I was at home. And I didn't realize what they were doing without, with my being unable to supply the emotional support they needed."

Elaine wishes she had known about such resources as Christian counseling, and "tough love" interventions to help the family of an alcoholic confront the problem. "I thought if I could be perfect, he would get better. I didn't want to admit that I was a failure as a wife."

She makes a suggestion. "I think it would be great if people would get regular marriage checkups like they get physical checkups. Then it wouldn't be admitting failure if you went to see someone. Everyone would be doing it; it would just be your six-month checkup. If we had done that, maybe a solution would have come to light sooner."

Of course, divorce changes the dynamics of relationships among the children involved and between the children and both spouses. In Elaine's case, "My older daughter became the mature person in the family. She would
make allowances and take care of things when I had a bad
day." It is also very likely that this daughter will resent
Mom for the times she sacrificed normal teenage activities
in order to tend to the family when her mother wasn't up
to it.

As Darrell, age sixteen, told an interviewer, "The hardest thing is that you have to take care of everybody—like
everybody wants a piece of you. I had to take care of my
little brothers (ages six, ten, and twelve) and my mother
after my father left. She was really upset and crying all the
time, and my little brothers didn't know what was going
on . . . it was a mess. I used to want to run away like my
father, but I couldn't because that would have killed my
mother. I was really mad at him for leaving. I guess I still
am, in a way."[5]

Divorce also jeopardizes future relationships for the
children involved. This is an iceberg, with much of the
damage potential hidden at the time of divorce. Dana F.
was so caught up in the tension of her relationship with
her husband that she could not see what was happening
to her children. Only when they grew up and began to
have trouble in their own marriages did Dana see that her
divorce caused them to mistrust the opposite sex.

Dana said, "I would change, if I could, the fact that I
told my oldest daughter all about my feelings of hate and
anger toward her father. She now has these same feelings
toward all men." The daughter is twenty-four.

Whether or not divorcing parents share their anger
about each other with their children, it's likely that the
children's future relationships will suffer. Researchers at
the University of Wisconsin project that 60 percent of recent marriages—which include more children of divorce
than ever before—will end in divorce. That's 10 percent
higher than the predictions of the last few years.[6] Although

other experts say the trauma of divorcing parents can help children learn from their parents' mistakes,[7] the facts seem to reduce their predictions to whistling in the dark.

A More Positive Way

Julio A. discovered something more positive about dealing with children when divorce is inevitable. Knowing the danger discussed above—"dumping" our anger on the kids or being painfully sure they know our side of the story—he would simply not discuss with his children the intimate details of his divorce. The fact is, their mother had abandoned them. But feeling that he must be at fault in some way, the children would get angry at him and use the "accusative case" in their tirades.

"But I would never put their mother down," he said. "No matter how angry the kids got, I'd just tell them, 'I love you.' And you know—lately my daughter has been able to see some of her mother's mistakes on her own, without my saying a word. And the other day she told me, 'Dad, if you weren't my father, I think I'd like to be married to you!' "

As Julio also points out, just as each parent is responsible only for his or her own behavior, not the spouse's, neither should a parent take on the responsibility of explaining a spouse's irresponsible behavior.

Too Late Young, Too Soon Old

The trauma of divorce makes some children revert to infantile behavior such as bedwetting. Ironically, it makes them grow old too soon as well, striking as a kind of Alzheimer's disease especially for kids.

Linda Bird Francke, a writer who specializes in women's and family issues, was prompted by her own divorce, and her children's reaction to it, to survey other children whose parents divorced. She found enough similarity among children of various age-groups that she was able to track typical responses, such as:

- Helplessness, typical of babies and toddlers.
- Guilt, typical of preschoolers.
- Sadness, in children ages six to eight.
- Anger among children nine to twelve.
- False maturity, among teenagers.[8]

This premature aging factor appeared more than once in a feature on children and divorce in *People* magazine.[9]

"You have to do more grown-up things," said Ryan, age nine, "and you have more grown-up feelings. It was easier when my dad was here." Some of the "grown-up" things Ryan has to do won't kill him—things like taking out the garbage and mowing the lawn. But who can assess the damage done when kids have to have certain kinds of feelings before they're ready to have them?

Blake, now twenty, recently dropped out of college—partly because he's learned too soon, from his parents' divorce ten years ago, that commitments can be broken. "I was committed to going to school. . . . If you say you are going to do something, and people are depending on you, then, yes, do it. But if it's something that can be flexible, like school or marriage. . . . "

Beth Harris also learned about flexible marriages from her parents and divorced her own husband after three years. "It was the way I knew how to cope with problems," she says. "It was easier for me to do because my parents had done it."

Sick of Divorce

Not only are children's emotions and psychological stability ravaged by divorce, but researcher Jane Mauldon of the University of California at Berkeley has linked divorce to children's physical health as well. According to her studies, children of divorce are nearly 10 percent more likely to develop health problems than other kids. The facts are clear enough to prompt some insurance companies to deny health insurance coverage for children of divorce, or to make it cost too much to buy.[10]

Of course, we cannot insure children against all the trauma of divorce. Often the most damage is done when parents are too caught up in their own relational pain to notice what's happening to the kids. Dana F. says, "When I was trying my own thing, my schedule didn't involve my children." Before she knew it, two of her four children were caught up in witchcraft; her twelve-year-old daughter told her she might need an abortion (she didn't, as it turned out, but she was sexually active), and another daughter reported that her father had fondled her. (Although he denied it, the symptoms of the girl's emotional trauma were obvious even if she invented the story.)

Dana began to try to correct her former neglect. "I tried to spend time with them before school and work," Dana said. "I played raquetball with the ten-year-old at 5:30 A.M." Obsessed with her weight, she would also jog a mile after work with her fourteen-year-old daughter. We understand when she adds, "I was a nervous wreck."

Two Strikes and Some Are Out

In the widely discussed book *Second Chances,* Judith Wallerstein and Sandra Blakeslee reveal the results of Wallerstein's ten-year study of the effects of divorce on men, women, and children. Her study showed that five years after divorce, more than one-third of the children were clinically depressed and functioning poorly—even though their custodial parent was in a second marriage. After ten years, 35 percent still had poor relationships with both parents, and 75 percent felt rejected and left out by their fathers.[11]

When such figures are cited, someone always asks whether similar dismal figures might not come from a study of children whose parents stay together unhappily. Isn't it as hard or harder on children to be subjected to

Mom and Dad's bickering and other mutual abuse in the home? Perhaps—but why limit the options to these two, both of which are strikes against children? A home filled with tension and bitterness is not the only alternative to divorce. The needs of children are reason enough to forge a new possibility: a marriage in which mutual acceptance overwhelms the differences that otherwise lead to fighting. That's the advice of counselor and columnist Eda LeShan:

> Like most of my colleagues in the 1950s and '60s, I rationalized that it was better for parents to divorce than for children to live in a war zone. Now I know those are not the only alternatives—there is a third, where caring adults work at becoming mature enough to learn to live together . . . without tormenting each other.[12]

LeShan has a poignant analogy from nature. She admits without shame to feeling a deep nostalgia when she sees a family of Canada geese—mother in front, father (with whom she has mated for life) watching the goslings from behind. The scene makes her long for "a time when human children were thus protected, one parent in front, one behind, a lifetime marriage!" LeShan knows that there are no perfect marriages, but asserts that "now we have better tools for clearing up the miseries—and we had better do it!"[13]

Children of Solomon's Court

Of all the effects of recent attempts to equalize divorce settlements, none is more damaging than the court-ordered treatment of children. As Solomon facetiously proposed, children are "sliced" precisely down their middles, one half going to the father and the other half to the mother.

A lovely, olive-skinned high school girl sat in my office, almost literally steaming. Her body language spoke volumes: arms folded tightly across her chest, jaw muscles taut, lower lip out. "I'm not going!" she said through clenched teeth.

"Going where?" I asked.

"To Dayton, to live with Dad."

"Don't you and your dad get along?"

"Of course we do," she returned, killing me with a withering glance. "But I like school here. And I just made cheerleader!"

Here was a girl at an age most sensitive to a move to another school, a girl who was "making it"—striving victoriously to overcome the effects of an unstable home with divorced parents—only to be ordered to divide her school year down the middle in order to keep her parents from feeling slighted or deprived of their rights.

This is only one of countless incidents that calls for the rights of children to be recognized in divorce settlements. The dilemma facing the courts, however, is that no-fault settlements mean that both father and mother have precisely equal rights that run squarely into what's best for the child. Too few divorcing parents are willing for the child to stay in the school near the ex-spouse's residence, even though the child is doing well. Horrors! That might signal the opposing spouse that he or she has won.

Toward Considering the Children

The disruption of a child's life by divorce is too serious for jokes, but the following story is real life, not a joke. Terry Hershey, widely known Christian author and speaker on relational issues, told in a speech of an elderly couple who petitioned a Los Angeles court for divorce. Upon inquiring, the judge learned that the man was ninety years old. Shocked, the judge asked the couple why they would call the marriage off this late in the game. At least their answer showed sensitivity to the problem this chapter addresses: "We had to wait for the children to die."

On a more serious note, several states have developed

special judicial processes in the hope of easing the impact of divorce courts on children. "Conciliation Courts" call on the aid of family counselors, psychologists, and social workers to help make custody arrangements, instead of leaving the issues to lawyers for warring parties. According to many authorities, this attempt to reduce the adversarial atmosphere surrounding custody decisions is working for the benefit of the children involved. The Divorce Mediation Center in Charlotte, North Carolina, has reported that 93 percent of the families who used the Center's mediation services expressed satisfaction with the results, compared to only 56 percent satisfaction reported by those who went through traditional adversarial channels.[14]

Such attempts to spare children the trauma of being pulled apart by divorcing parents are of course laudable. But they are still more oriented toward meeting the needs of parents than children. The simple fact is that the needs of the children are best met when parents stay together and work through their differences. If they would expend the amount of energy demanded to fight each other in the courts on the tough task of fighting their way through the jungle of jagged-edged relationships, they could save much more than a marriage. They could save countless children from becoming pawns — however enlightened — of a legal system that must act as family therapist.

Winning a Divorce, Losing a Child

Some courts are also taking a closer look at the traditional method of awarding custody to the mother instead of the father. But such reforms came too late for Clyde D. Here was another divorce that had every good reason to happen but was won with disastrous unforeseen regrets.

A strong Christian, Clyde was determined to marry someone who shared his faith. Sally assured him that she did. She used all the right evangelical terms about having asked Jesus into her heart. But while she had learned to talk the talk, she couldn't walk the walk. Only two weeks after her marriage—and during a church retreat—Sally boasted privately to some other women that she had deliberately deceived her new husband in her wedding vows: She had no intention of "forsaking all others."

The Christian network can be pretty tight, and Clyde found out what his new bride had said. Deeply hurt, of course, he nonetheless set about to salvage the marriage anyway. But without Sally's help, it was to no avail. She was involved with numerous other men during the eleven years he tried to hold the marriage together. After each revelation about another man in her life she would "repent," saying that Clyde was the only man she would ever really love, and vow anew to be faithful.

Then Sally got pregnant as the result of one more affair. Since she showed no remorse, Clyde felt he could do nothing but divorce her.

But what about their eight-year-old son Ernie? Clyde determined to obtain custody, on grounds that Sally's pregnancy proved she was an unfit mother. An attorney agreed to help him. But under pressure of the local, and very traditional, custody policy favoring mothers, the lawyer betrayed Clyde and his cause at the "eleventh hour." Sally won custody.

Ernie was thrown into a life in which he was surrounded by drug dependency and physical abuse. Nothing Clyde could say to the courts was as powerful as its bias toward "the superior nurturing quality" of a mother.

To be sure, Clyde sees his son Ernie frequently—in hearings where, in Clyde's words, "I defend him from his mother and various mental health professionals." In fact, Clyde has had to spend so much time in the political and judicial fallouts of his divorce that a new and special "someone" he hoped to marry issued an ultimatum: "It's either Ernie or me." Clyde had no alternative but to continue to fulfill his parental responsibility. He chose Ernie.

Now, lonely and bitter, Clyde can't say he regrets the divorce. What else could he do? But what "failed" about it—his plan to obtain custody of his son, and the life to which both he and his son have been consigned—has left him angry. "Ernie has been victimized by the system," Clyde says. "He has paid a tremendous price."

So has Clyde.

The Schools and the Four Rs

Many school-age children have two homes—the one they go to in the evening, and the school. The children of divorce, have three homes—school, the home of one parent, and the home of the other parent. It should be no surprise that the disruption of the primary home by divorce impacts the secondary home, the school.

Sensitive teachers feel they must now somehow communicate not only reading, writing, and arithmetic, but rehabilitation as well. While many teachers protest that this is an unfair burden on people and a system ill-prepared to deal with the fallout of divorce, all feel the effects of children whose schoolwork and attendance patterns are devastated by the disruptions and chaos at home.

Even seemingly small items become an issue. For example, where does a teacher send notes that relate to school activities? One teacher sent a note about what a little girl would need for Field Day to the girl's mother on Tuesday. But Field Day was on Thursday, and that was the day for the girl to be with her father. Not having the note, the father sent his daughter off to school where she found herself without jeans or parent or picnic. "It seems like a small thing," said the teacher, "but to her it was very big. She hid behind the bushes and cried until I found her."[15]

The impact of the recent research and such experiences as those reported here have yet to be fully assessed. In the last century, the discovery that children were being abused in sweatshops and other areas of the labor force raised such a cry that laws were enacted for their protection. Is it too much to hope that the sobs of children whose lives have been disrupted by divorce will also capture society's attention in the "sweatshop" environment of divorce?

CHAPTER FOUR

Adultery — and the One Thing Worse

illiam R. was part of a group of singles discussing with each other the burden of failed marriages — and some failed divorces. Divorced several months ago, William thought his marriage would have been the last one to break up. "I thought my marriage was like the *Titanic* — it would never go down," he said. "Even now, I can't accept the fact that it's over. Only a couple of weeks ago I was sitting on the bed with a shotgun aimed at my head. I wound up blowing a hole in the mattress, and it woke me up."

As you've already guessed from the title of this chapter, adultery — the source of some of the most unadulterated pain marriages can suffer — was what almost drove William to suicide. The irony is that he had thought his marriage was made in heaven. He recalls thinking, "The Lord put this marriage together, and no one could put it asunder. Whether we got along or didn't, God would keep the marriage together. We were both Christians and married before God and swore before God, and I assumed that eventually it would get itself straightened out. And it didn't."

Like many busy businessmen, William could not take time to tend to the growing discord he and his wife were experiencing. When they did take a few minutes to ac-

knowledge their difficulty, "We discussed separation a little, and even divorce, but I never took it seriously," he
said. "I thought it would fix itself. Later on in life, when
we got our finances together and our kids were grown,
we'd have more time to tend to the marriage."

Then he discovered his wife's unfaithfulness. "I can't
believe my wife was having an affair right under my nose—
and with one of my business associates! At first I pretend-
ed I didn't know what was going on. I should have been
wise enough to see what was going on rather than ignore
it and let things ferment."

The near miss William had with suicide is only one indication that it is hard to overstate the damage done to a
marriage by sexual unfaithfulness. The outrage, the feelings of rejection, the disillusionment, can knife like a sur-
geon's scalpel to the quick of the body-soul-spirit con-
glomerate we call persons. And it's a "procedure" that
happens without anesthesia. Perhaps that is why the Gospel of Matthew records Jesus as giving permission for divorce in cases of adultery (Matt. 5:32; 19:9)—an exception
to God's original intent that marriage be for life.[1]

A More Excellent Way

Ethel G.'s husband Joe had been unfaithful too. Once,
during a time in their marriage when he felt misunderstood, criticized, and unappreciated, Joe was called out of
town on business for extended periods. It was then that
he found the acceptance he wasn't feeling in his marriage—in another woman's arms.

If Joe and Ethel had assumed, as many couples do, that
adultery would absolutely end their marriage, they would
have divorced immediately. And it must be acknowledged,
in accord with Matthew's Gospel, that the wounds of adultery go so deep and the accompanying lies create so much
distrust that in some cases divorce is the only appropriate
response. Sometimes ending the marriage seems to be the
only adequate outlet for the natural outrage toward one

who has broken the vow to be faithful for life.

But Joe and Ethel had a second thought. They decided that the one thing that would hurt more than Joe's unfaithfulness would be divorcing because of it.

Unfortunately, many people have moved beyond the idea of adultery as a problem so serious as to prompt divine *permission* to divorce, to the assumption that divorce is virtually *required* when a spouse is unfaithful. The fact is that, like many others, Joe and Ethel discovered this natural reaction can lead to actually overstating the problem. They came to realize that hasty divorce after an affair can bring pain that goes deeper than the wound of sexual unfaithfulness.

Their pain, they learned, was *subjective,* as we noted in chapter 1. Somehow they fought through to an emotional place where they could be *objective* enough to see that the breach in their marriage could be contained to temporary status, while the pain of divorce would last much longer. Adultery was a serious wound to their relationship, but Joe and Ethel determined that it need not be fatal. It brutally cut away some cherished portions of their relationship, but they decided against the sharper pain of amputation.

We are not speaking here of "overlooking" adultery as though it were a minor breach in the marriage vows, or of living in a situation where unfaithfulness continues. Denial or pandering to perversion is not a successful way to deal with adultery. One woman—a devout Christian—was hoodwinked into the proverbial *ménage á trois,* tolerating a third party in bed with her husband and herself. Painful or not, divorce is a highly appropriate way to deal with a spouse who insists on such an arrangement on an ongoing basis.

In fact, ironically, some outrage is often a necessary stage of any attempt to prevent adultery from destroying a marriage. While it may be human to err and divine to forgive, divorce in cases of adultery is not successfully avoided by trying too hard, too quickly, to be divine.

A Storm Can Clear the Air

Ethel came close to making the mistake of acting too "godlike." Joe, who is a Christian, was overcome with remorse when he admitted his escapade to his wife. Although shocked and hurt, Ethel was "too good a Christian" to storm out of the house. Because Joe had recently been so unhappy in the marriage, she was afraid that such a display of anger would drive him away for good.

Also, Ethel still loved Joe. She knew that he was devastated by what he had done. So she began earnestly and immediately reassuring him that the incident need not be the end of their marriage. She did everything "right" — she told him she forgave him, she tried hard to be less critical, she made herself very available to him sexually.

Suddenly, *Joe* left home.

Why? Despite his moral lapse, Joe was still so morally sensitive that Ethel's quickness to smooth over the incident somehow didn't fit the crime. His already shaky moral framework was thrown even further askew. His adultery had shattered his confidence that there were any moral foundations in his life, any real rights and wrongs to bring stability again to his world. Perhaps *God* could forgive him (although he was none too sure of that). But Ethel, after all, was only human. Her quick eagerness to forgive made him uneasy at first, then strangely angry. For him, infidelity deserved moral outrage. He was outraged with himself— why wasn't Ethel equally upset?

Struggling for an answer, Joe interpreted Ethel's "easy forgiveness" as desperate dependence — an attempt to keep him at any cost. Apparently she would do anything— even overlook adultery—to hang on to him. But her dependency was one of the very frustrations Joe had struggled with before his escapade. That, together with the fact that she now appeared to him to be literally too good to be true, made him feel smothered. So he recoiled from her touch as she reached out in forgiveness.

Eventually Ethel came across the "tough love" approach

advocated by such counseling professionals as Dr. James Dobson.[2] She realized that while she could not fake tough- ness when she really felt forgiving, Joe did need to see some moral stability in his wife. For one thing, after losing his own moral compass, he needed to be reassured that *someone* in the family had not lost hers. He may even have needed—rightly or wrongly from a theological view- point—to feel a little punished. Mainly, however, Ethel needed to affirm her self-worth with a little moral outrage. Fortunately, she reached a point of personal strength. When blended with her love for Joe, this enabled her to say, "I love you and I want our marriage to last. But if you don't love me enough to honor your marriage vows, I can make it on my own."

Suddenly Joe was able to look at Ethel in a new light. Since people with self-worth are more attractive than those who think they're not worthy to take a stand, Joe found his smothered feelings giving way to renewed re- spect—even admiration. Here was a woman who not only was strong enough to forgive, but also could live without him. Joe wanted the new Ethel. He came home.

Another potential divorce had failed to develop.

Ethel now advises the "offended party" in cases of adul- tery not to be too quick to reassure the offender nothing is wrong. *Of course* something is wrong! In such situations, it's as futile to be soft and passive and over-forgiving as it is to automatically shout, "I'm divorcing you!" A spouse so offended, she says, might well storm out of the house and spend some time away. It will not only afford some healthy ventilation to natural anger, but it may be just the kind of response that will help an offending mate do some essen- tial grief work over an action he or she may really regret as much as the offended spouse regrets it.

Is the "Innocent Party" Guiltless?

"Tough love" should not be interpreted as an excuse to recoil from an adulterous mate as though he or she had become untouchable. It's understandable when the spouse who hasn't been sexually unfaithful reacts this way—that's why the old term "the offended party" communicates so quickly and clearly. But understandable or not, it's not very helpful. The term hints at an attitude that is ruinous to attempt to stay together—the attitude that "the offended party" bears no guilt for the problem, and that the only offense lies with the adulterous spouse.

This is not a plea to excuse adultery on the grounds that "there are two sides to every argument," or to play down its potential disastrous effects on marriage. We've already seen that attempting to justify adultery by pretending the "guilty party" isn't really guilty skews the moral framework of marriage. This *is* a plea to recognize that a marriage struggling to survive adultery can rarely be rescued without addressing the issue of the *faithful* partner's attitudes and behavior. Often it is only after a divorce that this partner, while sexually faithful, can admit that he or she was hardly perfect.

Dorothy S. looked back after divorcing her husband for adultery. She had every *right* to leave, biblically and legally. Now, however, she says sadly, "I know now that I shouldn't have left. There are things I could have done differently. I regret not standing by Gene in his time of need."

Surely this kind of confession represents a mature and balanced sense of morality. Dorothy is not saying that her husband's adultery was "her fault." She is simply recognizing that few offenses occur in a vacuum. She now realizes that her husband's unfaithfulness was not only a moral lapse or sin; it represented profound needs that she wishes she had helped meet.

Psychologist April Westfall tries to get couples with this problem to talk about their marriage in terms broader than the act of adultery:

> I try to put the affair in the context of the entire marriage. If I can get them to see that this is like

other crises they have dealt with, such as job disruptions, ill children, the death of relatives, couples can be reminded of their resilience. It tends to
make them feel more hopeful and that there is a
possibility they can get through this.[4]

Probing in such areas often indicates that the "innocent" party is merely innocent of adultery; that he or she
is in fact at fault in some way that helped "set up" the
offender. Responsibility for contributing to a *situation*
that led to adultery can be admitted without accepting
false blame for the adulterous *response* to the situation.

For Ethel and Joe, hours of counseling for Ethel showed
her that her hypercriticism and need to control her husband contributed to the desperate, trapped feeling he experienced in the marriage. She resisted accepting this responsibility for months because to her it was the same as
saying she was responsible for Joe's actions. All the while,
Joe was feeling "one down." It seemed to him that Ethel
thought that he bore all responsibility for their marriage
problems because his was "the greater sin." When she was
able to slice through the complex issues more objectively,
and with sharper moral perceptivity, she could admit her
shortcomings which had been such a problem for her husband. With *her* confession, Joe was able to take full responsibility for the adultery itself.

Ethel's situation implies that adultery is not the only way
to break a marriage vow. Few *consequences* of undue criti-
cism aimed at a spouse are more harmful than sexual infidelity. But both lapses are a part of the brokenness and
imperfections of flawed human beings; and until both can
at least be considered in the same moral framework, the
"worse" moral lapse resists healing.

One woman who was having an affair went to counseling with her husband merely to prepare him for divorce.
"After a few sessions," she says, "I realized that I wasn't
really feeling numb as I had thought for at least a year. I
was in a total rage at my husband for the previous *four*

years because of his singular devotion to his business."
Finally realizing that his wife's unfaithfulness wasn't the
only thing wrong with their marriage, her husband woke
up and began to work on himself. Then they were able to
continue in counseling—in order to stay together instead
of to divorce.⁴

Poet Ella Wheeler Wilcox wrote movingly from the viewpoint of "an offending party," pleading for a reexamina-
tion not just of her unfaithfulness but of the entire context
in which it occurred:

AN UNFAITHFUL WIFE TO HER HUSBAND
Branded and blackened by my own misdeeds
I stand before you; not as one who pleads
For mercy or forgiveness, but as one,
After a wrong is done,
Who seeks the why and wherefore.
                                              Go with me,
Back to those early years of love, and see
Just where our paths diverged. You must recall
Your wild pursuit of me, outstripping all
Competitors and rivals, till at last
You bound me sure and fast
With vow and ring.
I was the central thing
In all the Universe for you just then.
Just then for me, there were no other men.
I cared
Only for tasks and pleasures that you shared.
Such happy, happy days. You wearied first.
I will not say you wearied, but a thirst
For conquest and achievement in man's realm
Left love's barque with no pilot at the helm.
The money madness, and the keen desire
To outstrip others, set your heart on fire.
Into the growing conflagration went
Romance and sentiment.
Abroad you were a man of parts and power—

Your double dower
Of brawn and brains gave you a leader's place;
At home you were dull, tired, and commonplace.
You housed me, fed me, clothed me; you were
   kind;
But oh, so blind, so blind.
You could not, would not, see my woman's need
Of small attentions; and you gave no heed
When I complained of loneliness; you said,
"A man must think about his daily bread
And not waste time in empty social life—
He leaves that sort of duty to his wife
And pays her bills, and lets her have her way,
And feels she should be satisfied."
                         Each day,
Our lives that had been one life at the start,
Farther and farther seemed to drift apart.
Dead was the old romance of man and maid.
Your talk was all of politics or trade.
Your work, your club, the mad pursuit of gold
Absorbed your thoughts. Your duty kiss fell cold
Upon my lips. Life lost its zest, its thrill.
                             Until
One fateful day when earth seemed very dull
It suddenly grew bright and beautiful.
I spoke a little, and he listened much;
There was attention in his eyes, and such
A note of comradeship in his low tone,
I felt no more alone.
There was a kindly interest in his air;
He spoke about the way I dressed my hair.
And praised the gown I wore.
It seemed a thousand, thousand years and more
Since I had been so noticed. Had mine ear
Been used to compliments year after year,
If I had heard you speak
As this man spoke, I had not been so weak.
The innocent beginning

Of all my sinning
Was just the woman's craving to be brought
Into the inner shrine of some man's thought.
You held me there, as sweetheart and as bride;
And then as wife, you left me far outside.
So far, so far, you could not hear me call;
You might, you should, have saved me from my fall.
I was not bad, just lonely, that was all.

A man should offer something to replace
The sweet adventure of the lover's chase
Which ends with marriage. Love's neglected laws
Pave pathways for the "Statutory Cause."⁵

"Working" Doesn't Mean Drudgery

It is often said that good marriages take work. If that's so,
marriages in which adultery has occurred take more work.
Interviews and studies show that there must be some fundamental changes in the marriage that survives adultery.
We have noticed how it helps for the "offended" party to
be willing to change anything that may have contributed to
the adultery. There can be no illusions about "things remaining the same." The marriage must now become the
scene of "emotional work."

Lucy W. met with a group of friends, all of whose husbands had been unfaithful. They assessed the pros and
cons of divorce but decided "to try to sort things out,"
instead. But things had to change.

> There was no going back to how it was. The stress
> is, indeed, on "making transparent" the relation-
> ship and discussing everything—in order to achieve
> a new and more mature intimacy.⁶

As Joe and Ethel found, intimacy really is possible, even
after adultery. But it has to be rebuilt with patience. For
example, the "offended party" may have to tolerate the

offender's occasional impotence. A spouse may sometimes even feel that "the other woman" (or man) is in bed with them. Make no mistake: It *is* work to struggle through that kind of scene.

Unfortunately, the notion of working at a relationship is interpreted by some to mean that the couple can no longer have fun or enjoy spontaneity in their marriage. One researcher concluded that the couples she interviewed who were working on a marriage flawed by adultery had given up on fun.[7] Such an attitude poses false either/or alternatives: either divorce and possibly have marital fun again, or hang onto your marriage grimly with no hope for any more hilarity.

But many couples have found that *divorce,* not working on a marriage, is the real threat to fun in their lives. So they take on the tough task of rebuilding their marriage because they know that after adultery *any* intimacy would take work. And couples who have the patience and love to negotiate this difficult passage know that a relationship is not depleted of fun just because it requires extra work.

Steps toward a Solution

Marriage counselor J. Allan Petersen has had wide experience working with couples who seemed to be headed for divorce because of adultery. In his book, *The Myth of Greener Grass,* Petersen isolates ten practical principles that have helped those whose partners have been unfaithful deal with the painful blow.[8]

1. *Take time before you take action.* Otherwise, you will act only out of explosive emotions, untempered by reason.

2. *Separate the facts from your opinions*—so you can act on the facts instead of your angry opinion about them.

3. *Don't let the present destroy the past.* Ask yourself if the immediate deception really means "He (or she) never really loved me."

4. *Commit yourself to learn—not to leave.* The crisis

certainly pinpoints a need. But can that be a catalyst for change instead of doom for the marriage?

5. *Determine the facts before deciding the fate.* A one-night stand might call for a different course of action than an illicit relationship that went on for ten years.

6. *Ask for reasons, not details.* Reasons can help you see whether you can change anything in your own behavior that needs changing. Insisting on details ("Did you ever have her here in our house, in our bed?") might bring needless hurt at a time when your pain threshold is low.

7. *Increase your growth, not your guilt.* Don't buy future pangs of guilt by divorcing before you've given your best shot at personal examination and growth.

8. *Allow each partner to own his own actions.* Remember that while your partner is responsible for his actions, you are responsible for your reaction.

9. *Share with a confidant or counselor.* See if another person's feedback points to a solution which you've been unable to see through your tears.

10. *Seek your forgiveness, then speak your forgiveness.* Neither adultery nor any way you may have contributed to your partner's unhappiness in the marriage is the unforgivable sin.

Without question, infidelity can enshroud a marriage in devastating darkness. Being able to focus on such beacons and guidelines as these offered by Petersen requires a special kind of vision—the ability to chop the devastating event itself down to size, and the ability to view it not as the primary problem in the marriage but as a symptom that something else has gone wrong.

PART II

Countering Cultural Myths about Divorce

Remember the counterculture? Young adults of the '60s and '70s challenged the values of an entire society. It's time for another cultural revolution—one that takes on the glib myths that tell us not to feel guilty, that marriage problems are our partner's fault, and that if the relationship isn't perfect, it should be scrapped.

CHAPTER FIVE

For Heaven's Sake

any of the regrets about divorce revealed in my survey stemmed from guilt. Even in cases that clearly called for divorce, many people carried in their hearts the suspicion that they had done wrong.

One woman explained that her guilt extends into the way divorce now requires her to live. "I go constantly," she says, and expresses guilt for not having provided her children with the normal quota of two parents—an arrangement that, as every single parent knows, enables us to send substitutes in for each other before we're too exhausted to play the game any more.

A forty-four-year-old woman divorced for six years still feels guilty for having so little patience with her husband. Six months after her divorce she had a change of heart and told her ex-husband that the divorce was a mistake; but by then he was already living with a nineteen-year-old girl. Now she says, "I felt so guilty for ruining my husband's life . . . and my children are a mess."

Sources of Shame

Because Malachi 2:16 clearly quotes God as saying, "I hate divorce," it's certainly understandable when people who take God's view seriously feel guilty about severing the marriage bond. But why do so many non-Christian people also suffer guilt when they divorce?

In the past sociologists might have answered that guilt is merely a social construct—we experience shame only because those around us say, "For shame!" It would be hard to take such a superficial answer seriously today. With half the new marriages in our society ending in divorce, it's fairly clear that the social stigma divorce once had has disappeared. Even conservative churches, who take very seriously the fact that God hates divorce, now have ministries for divorced people and preach against treating them as social lepers.

The fact is, it's been decades since divorce carried enough stigma to instill "socially constructed" guilt. The whole tenor of society has shifted in the opposite direction. Almost overnight our culture has gone from branding divorced people with a shameful *D* to fully accepting divorce as a normal way of life.

And what's wrong with that? Should we revert to whispering about divorced people and ostracizing them from polite society? Certainly not. In the first place, that's no way to treat people who hurt, whether they've handled the hurt appropriately or not. Secondly, there is no longer the presumed majority of the undivorced "we" to render such judgments. "We" are among the divorced! In fact, one reason society has tried so hard to eliminate the social stigma divorce once carried is that so many of the shapers of society are divorced themselves.

Isn't it interesting that so many people have flown in the face of society's recent pressure to normalize divorce—by going ahead and feeling guilty anyway? Again, what is the source of this stubbornly persistent shame?

A Genetic Memory?

This situation invites the conclusion that the idea of marriage to one person for a lifetime is a kind of gene implanted so deeply within the makeup of both believers and unbelievers that ignoring the gene can set up shock waves of guilt that can crack the depths of our being.

This gene did not develop from Christianity, and it's even older than Judaism. In fact, it's as old as Creation, when God made man and woman "in Our image." (See Gen. 1:26.) Without getting into a Bible study here, we should note that people created in the image of God reflect God's primary attributes — "in this world we are like Him" (1 John 4:17). And what is the one trait attributed to God above all others in the Bible? It's the one confessed in the ancient Jewish "Shemah" — "Hear O Israel: the Lord our God, the Lord is *one*" (Deut. 6:4, emphasis mine).

Now add to this truth the biblical idea that in marriage, man and woman become "one." The implication is that *the union of two people in marriage reflects the unity or oneness of God.* Unfortunately, the breakup of a marriage is a reflection on God also — a false reflection. *The divorce of two married people makes the false claim that God is not one after all,* because people are made "in His image."

No wonder divorce can create guilt! Whether or not we believe in God with conscious assent, we must "believe" from the genes up. Our very makeup cries out against "putting asunder" what God has joined together — it is damaging both to people and to the concept of God it projects.

Feelings of shame are also natural because keeping promises is a universal value — not just a Christian teaching. Staying married to the person we promised to stay married to is therefore a *structural* issue. Even when circumstances *require* us to break a promise, we are likely to feel guilty because we know we're having to take a step we can't recommend as ideal. And when those feelings of guilt are overlooked or treated lightly — even by well-meaning people trying to move beyond the judgmentalism of the past — our very souls protest.

Principles vs. People

Of course what society does with such protests is something else. We do have the awful freedom to go against our inner objections, though not without cost. And when people widely ignore the ideal in favor of particular exceptions to the rule, God's way loses its social support.

Widespread unbelief, of course, undermines the support society formerly gave to staying married. So does the elevation of individualism and privatism in our day. In *Divorced in America,* Joseph Epstein notes that divorce mirrors a general decline in the credibility of both religion and community. Our incredibly high divorce rate accompanies both a decline in faith that God expects people to do His will, and in the power of the believing community to provide the glue that once helped keep families together.[1]

This is not an appeal to go back to ostracizing the divorced. As in the case of the woman caught in the act of adultery, Jesus Himself made people a higher priority than the law. (See John 8:1-11.) The strides toward accepting divorced people in recent years, and not holding it against children that their parents are divorced, are steps forward, not backward. But the fact that so many divorced people experience unexpected guilt raises the question: Has compassion and fair play toward *people* who divorce caused us to condone divorce itself as an act that has no moral dimensions? If so, it's not a sign that we've grown more ethically sophisticated so much as an indication that we are making light of the guilty feelings many divorced people continue to experience.

Jeffrey T. certainly doesn't want his Christian friends to return to the "scarlet letter" treatment of divorced people, but he still wants to discuss it within a moral framework. "I was a workaholic," he confesses, "and I was also addicted to my wife. I lost both of them. I want to plug [being in] groups where you can at least talk about problems like this, and not be evaluated, and interrupted by people telling you what you're doing wrong, [but] you can talk about it as Christians, and you can pray about it."

Such divorced people have fought their way through issues of guilt and grace to the point that they show a much greater moral sensitivity than those who wink at divorce. They have learned to face their own faults and to bring them to God. For them, the process of repentance has brought a sense of healing and forgiveness they could never have realized had they listened to those who want to overlook the moral dimensions of divorce.

What does "the process of repentance" mean?

Calling Sin Sin

You have already met Carl Adamson, the minister who almost divorced. As we might expect, moral constraints were part of what made him fight so long and hard to save his own marriage. He was fortunate enough to have two friends who took his sense of guilt seriously. They allowed him to experience it, instead of saying, "Don't feel guilty."

"They pointed out that the direction I was headed was wrong," he recalled, "which I needed to hear. That explicit word needed to be said. However long it takes to sink in, it has to be said. Sin needs to be named *sin,* and a way of living that is the way of repentance needs to be pointed out. Basically, they told me to resign my position [as a minister—see chapter 8] and work on my marriage."

I asked Carl to explain the moral framework in which he now does marriage counseling. How does he handle guilty feelings? Does he deal with divorce as a "sin," as his friends did?

"Divorce is never 'right,' " he said. "Divorce is always sin, it's always a violation of God's plan. But there are times when it's necessary. The same is true in reference to killing a person. Killing is always wrong; it's always a sin. But there are times when it's necessary, as in war, or defending your family. There are times when it's necessary because we live in a fallen world."

Knowing that some Christian counselors with this view assert that people should not divorce, even when they are being abused in their marriage, I asked him about cases like that.

"I would say, 'Don't stay there, don't take abuse,' " Carl replied, "but I would also say, 'Don't get divorced. Let him divorce you. Let him fire the first shot.'

"Abuse is a part of our world system that 'forces' people to get divorced. God's system holds us together. It's the human system, the secular system, that forces divorce or creates the possibilities for divorce."

"Then would people who decide they simply *must* divorce leave a counseling session with you burdened with guilt?" I asked.

"In my view," he answered, "they're going to go away much more dependent on the cross of Jesus Christ than they were before they came in. Divorce in our culture, perhaps more than anything else, gives us the opportunity for self-justification. Individuals try to justify themselves, justify their divorce. I mean, we're bright people. We will find ways to weasel our way into sin, and to feel justified for it.

"But the Apostle John says, 'If we claim to be without sin, we deceive ourselves and the truth is not in us.' [See 1 John 1:8.] For people to recognize the sin of their divorce only throws them more completely on the Cross for forgiveness in Jesus Christ. I believe there are times when we need to be like Job—alone before God, sitting on the ash heap of our lives in dust and ashes, with the soot of repentance on our faces."

In Carl's view, this approach enables people he counsels to leave his office having found the answer to guilt, rather than being burdened by it, "because they find their sole dependence upon Christ and His righteousness." But he insisted that "the double-edged sword of the Gospel has to be a part of it—one edge being judgment and the other edge forgiveness.

"It seems to me that God doesn't wink at divorce," he

continued. "He didn't wink at that which sent Jesus to the cross—any more than He winks at cheating on taxes—because that too sent Jesus to the cross. What we have to proclaim, when we say that divorce is necessary, is that because we live in a fallen world, we sometimes participate in sin. But let's not deceive ourselves by saying that we don't sin. We sin. As Martin Luther said, in some cases we sin boldly, that grace may abound."

Carl's words are echoed in a passage from Sharon Marshall's book, *Separation and Divorce*:

> Wholeness will come when you acknowledge your part in the failure of your marriage—however unintentional it may have been—and allow God to transform you so you don't end up in the same situation again (our past has a strange way of repeating itself).[2]

Dana F. found this to be the truth. Struggling with guilt, as mentioned above, she finally brought it to the feet of Him who alone is strong enough to bear it. "I cried, 'God help me and tell me what to do!' " In her case the answer was "realizing that God loved me and wanted me to have the power—His power, and His strength—to overcome my problems." She is convinced that this experience would not have happened had she not been deeply penitent for her part in the failure of her marriage. Now she can speak of "the washing of the Word," and of "forgetting what is behind and straining toward what is ahead" (Phil. 3:13).

Intervention and Its Risk

Carl Adamson's strong views have led him into a ministry of intervention in connection with marriage problems—an approach similar to that used in some cases of alcohol and drug abuse. He and his wife Katie have gone into homes to intervene when a divorce seemed imminent, sometimes confronting a spouse face-to-face with how he or she is contributing to the breakdown of the marriage.

"I view it as something like the time when Christ said if you have something against your brother you go to him, and if he won't repent, take a witness with you and again call on him to repent. And when we talk about repentance, we're not talking about feeling sorry, but *turning* — changing one's mind and behavior, which is the biblical sense of the word."

As I suspected, such boldness doesn't always win friends; but the desire to be "liked" isn't as strong in Carl as his conviction that a part of his role is to save marriages, not officiate at divorces. Once he and his wife marched into a home and told a husband some things his wife had shared with Carl in counseling—things that were about to wreck the marriage. "We took the chance of being rejected, of losing these people from the church," he said, "but that's fine if they stay together. If they will just soften up enough to let God work in their lives, I have no doubt that their marriage will be saved. And they'll realize that as painful as it was, it was this kind of surgery that healed them."

The Role of Rules

Many people would be scandalized by Belinda M.'s determination to stay married primarily because of her conviction that divorce is against God's rules. She was separated from her husband Dennis, who seemed to think that divorce was inevitable. The marriage was far from perfect for both, but Belinda believed that the pain of marriage was far less than the pain of defying the rules.

Such an attitude is widely dismissed today as "legalism." Doesn't following *rules* that closely risk hurting *people?* And shouldn't we put people before rules? Such questions pose a false choice and false alternatives. Belinda refuses to pit people and rules against each other. The rules, she argues, are *for* people. It's *breaking* them that hurts people.

"I just didn't like the thought of living under the rule that rules don't count," Belinda explained. "We make wedding vows to make the marriage secure against the times we just don't feel good about things. The wedding license—it's like a birth certificate that protects the rights of an infant against capricious acts. My covenant with my husband was made to protect us against whimsy and caprice too. I just prefer that to living only under the rule that you can do anything you feel like doing at the moment."

When Belinda and Dennis' separation dissolved, and they got back together, they found that this allegiance to the rules in no way took the spontaneity and zest out of their relationship as so many think it might. They created a new romance out of the rubble of the old. Dennis credits it largely to his wife's insistence that they should stick to the rules. For her part, Belinda confesses that she has another love in her life besides Dennis. She also loves to keep the rules.

Robert H.'s experience was similar, except he and his wife divorced. Their stormy relationship when they were first married led to a divorce. Later, Robert became a Christian. It changed him so much that his wife wanted to get back together with him. Unfortunately, they had not resolved their differences, and the marriage was again extremely painful.

"I couldn't initiate a divorce as a Christian," Robert said. "I had to bite my tongue and trust the Lord." But his wife, who was not a Christian, left, and divorced him. Robert now cites 1 Corinthians 7:15: "But if the unbeliever leaves, let him do so. A believing man or woman is not bound in such circumstances." He says he could not have lived at peace with himself had he initiated divorce.

Facing Both the Real and the Ideal

Many Christians who have divorced want more than anything that God's ideal of one man and one woman for life be upheld. Some simply will not attend a church where this message isn't preached—even if this means risking some leftover guilty feelings. While this requires a great deal of sensitivity, it's actually what all of us must do: repent and accept God's forgiveness for sins past, while upholding God's ideal for the present and the future.

Bible expositor John Stott points out the fact that because we fall short of the ideal doesn't mean we should abandon the *intention* of "living God's way to the hilt." Christ's emphasis in His teaching about divorce upheld the ideal. Possible exceptions to the ideal are limitless, and to put our emphasis there in order to salve our wounds will lead us to miss the point that others can be spared such pain if the ideal is upheld.

> If we allow ourselves to become preoccupied with divorce and its grounds, rather than marriage and its ideals, we lapse into pharisaism. God's purpose is marriage, not divorce, and His gospel is good news of reconciliation.[5]

Several of the persons interviewed for this book added a very practical point they wished people considering divorce could hear: *Even if divorce is necessary, don't demean yourself by saying and doing things you wish you could take back.* That just compounds the guilt factor, creating a monster that will rise up to haunt you later.

"Be fair!" said Billie R. "Remember that the other person is also hurting. Everything you feel, he feels too."

"Don't get so wrapped up in yourself and your needs that you can't consider your children's feelings, and those of your spouse," said a forty-four-year-old divorcée mentioned earlier.

And we might also remember the collective counsel of many divorced people who also warn against getting so wrapped up in our pain that we can't consider how God feels about divorce. Only when divorce is treated this seriously can we speak of Christ's forgiving grace. To treat divorce flippantly or to view it as having no moral consequence is not only to discount the very real guilt feelings so many divorced people have, but it is also to treat Christ's cross flippantly. Grace is free, but it wasn't cheap. We rejoice in God's power to forgive even the murderer, but we don't condone murder. Millions of us also rejoice that God can forgive us for breaking our marriage vows. But the point here is that there can be no rejoicing, only unatoned guilt, when breaches in God's Law prompt only cover-ups, instead of repentance.

CHAPTER SIX

I Have Met the Enemy— and It Wasn't My Spouse

n old story has it that a man saw his doctor because he was constantly wheezing, complained of a sore throat, had a tingling in his arms and legs, and saw spots before his eyes. After exhaustive diagnoses, the doctor decided to amputate the man's left leg. Still he suffered all the symptoms. The doctor took off his right leg . . . then one arm . . . and finally the other arm . . . all to no avail. Giving up on life in general and doctors in particular, the poor man had himself rolled into a men's store. He would purchase one last suit of clothes—at least he could be buried in style.

"What size shirt do you need?" asked the salesman, measuring the unfortunate man's neck as he spoke.

"Size fourteen," wheezed the doomed man.

"What?" the salesman exclaimed. "Why, you have a size sixteen neck!"

"No way," insisted the ailing man. "I've always purchased a size fourteen shirt. Now don't give me a hard time. Give a dying man his last request. Just sell me a fourteen shirt."

"All right," the salesman said, reluctantly. "If that's what you want, that's what you get—but I'm warning you: it'll give you a sore throat, and make you wheeze and tingle and see spots before your eyes."

Thousands of people amputate their spouse in divorce with the mistaken view that he or she is the problem.

When Differences Weren't the Problem

Jamie and Millie had little going for their marriage. Millie felt that Jamie had no respect for her, and they were simply too different to live together. They had been separated more than once, and during the last separation Millie had decided, finally, to get a divorce. But one day a mutual friend told me that it hadn't worked out that way. Jamie and Millie were together again, and I wanted to find out why.

After only fifteen minutes in their home, I could tell what they meant when they said they were different. Jamie is a retired Navy captain, still trim and fit at over sixty, with close-clipped hair and military precision in his step. "I'm a pretty organized person," he offered. I saw his point when the clock struck eight. "Well—time for the cats to go out," he said, getting up from his recliner. He looked at his watch. "Let's see—they'll need to be let in at nine. They stay out one hour."

All right. Precisely one hour for the cats.

What about Millie? She isn't as trim as Jamie and is more relaxed. "I'm as disorganized as Jamie is organized," she said. An art major years ago, Millie still uses her artistic abilities to decorate their modest home tastefully.

But here they were, describing each other's differences with chuckles and winks. After saying how overorganized Jamie is, Millie added, "And I'm so much the opposite I need someone like that." And Jamie said proudly, "I didn't see much in this house when we first looked at it, but Millie walked in and sized up the place and saw its potential—and look how nice she's made it."

What had enabled this couple to view their differences as fortunate complements instead of aggravating opposites? Why had their anticipated divorce failed to materialize?

The Kids Wouldn't Let Us

"Well," Millie sighed, tucking her short legs under her on the deep-cushioned couch, "I guess you could say we just put it off too long. And besides—our kids wouldn't let us."

"Are you serious?" I asked, knowing that their children are all grown and gone.

"Sure," Millie replied. "They just sat us down and told us that they didn't want the hassle of having to visit us separately on holidays. So we just kept putting the divorce off while we worked on our drinking problem and I got my business going—and after awhile we couldn't see any reason to put the kids out so."

Of course the real reasons behind both the marital stress and the reunion were coming out now. It had little to do with their differing personalities. Two other problems—alcoholism and Millie's low self-esteem—had masqueraded as marriage problems. When they were able to conquer their drinking problem, and when Millie learned that she could support herself if she had to, they had no need to divorce. Fortunately, Millie and Jamie diagnosed the real problem before severing their relationship.

"For years we were so full of booze we really didn't know what we were arguing about," Jamie said. But however undefined their arguments were when they were under the influence, the alcohol heightened Jamie's ability to put Millie down. Feeling like "dirt," it was Millie who first decided she was so sick of herself that she would change. With the help of Alcoholics Anonymous, she stopped drinking.

Ironically, that's when she first decided to get a divorce. Actually, it's fairly common for alcoholics to divorce when one of them sobers up. "I could see what he was doing to me for the first time," Millie said. She took their case to a marriage counselor, blaming their failing marriage on the fact that Jamie would not stop drinking as she had. She was taken aback when the counselor told her she was half the problem. Typically, she had begun to "enable" her husband to keep drinking by her continued nagging.

But Millie kept talking with her counselor. She faced what she had to face in herself. But Jamie could not; the counseling sessions failed to bring them together.

Still, Millie could not bring herself to leave. Jamie supported them comfortably, with the $400 a week pension he received as a former Navy captain. She had devoted her married life to raising four boys, and now she had no idea what marketable skills she might use to make a living. She was frankly afraid to divorce.

The Enabler Moves Out

Then an opportunity came for her to sell cosmetics through a home service plan. She started the program tentatively but was surprised to discover she was good at it. The company noticed too. When they promised to train her for a managerial position if she would move, she jumped at the chance. The move would relieve the tension in the marriage and also help Millie develop the ability to support herself. She moved. They were separated.

Millie's move suited Jamie fine, at first. It saved him the trouble of leaving. Then a new problem appeared: He was faced with being a single parent. "The trouble was, I didn't even know my own kids," Jamie admits. "I'd left all the parenting to Millie." When he discovered that one of the boys was on drugs, he was beside himself. He got the boy into a drug program, only to be told that he needed it as much as his son, for alcoholism. He decided that if it would help his boy whip the drug problem, he would try it.

It worked—for both.

Getting his head on straighter allowed Jamie to get all the kids graduated from home. He joined Millie in the nearby city where she was being trained. They still were too far apart to make it work and went to more intensive counseling.

Now Millie learned that she had been a passive, "why does everything happen to me?" kind of person. Partly because of her new job skills, she discovered that she had more control over her life than she thought. If she and Jamie divorced, it would be the result of a rational decision, not a "poor-me" burden dumped on her. Now both she and Jamie were freer than ever to make choices independent of drink and the "poor-me's."

Of course these two freed-up people were now much more attractive than they had been as victims. With their newly cleared vision, they began to see why they had been attracted to each other in the beginning. They chose to allow their separation to fail, instead of their marriage.

When Divorce Won't Help

The story of Jamie and Millie illustrates a basic truth many people learn only after one or more divorces. It was stated crisply years ago in the title of a book on divorce written by a psychiatrist, Dr. Edmund Beagler. He called his book simply *Divorce Won't Help*. After years of treating hundreds of couples, Dr. Beagler concluded that divorce was simply an unconscious way to perpetuate a neurosis. Conflict between spouses actually masked conflicts within each spouse. Instead of dealing with the real issues within themselves, couples fight each other. After all, if they stopped to allow the unconscious to come to light, they would have to give up some of their favorite habits, such as blaming others or feeling sorry for themselves.

So the tension escalates, Dr. Beagler maintained, until "one marriage partner sacrifices the other to retain the possibility of repeating this inner conflict with somebody else."[1] Since the first marriage had not provided a means of continuing a neurotic pattern without being challenged, a second might, our neuroses tell us; and so the cycle is repeated.

Alcoholism was obviously one neurotic symptom in both Jamie's and Millie's personalities. In Millie's case, learned helplessness was also a factor. Had they not delayed divorce until those personal issues could be settled, Dr.

Beagler would have predicted that they would seek out a subsequent relationship to feed their neurosis—with equally disastrous results.

Any Cause Will Do

Family systems experts Augustus Napier and Carl Whitaker have probed this tendency to select grounds for divorce that are mere masks of deeper inner conflicts. In their experience, the partner who has decided that he or she simply *must* leave feels threatened with "engulfment," while the partner pleading for the other to stay feels threatened with "abandonment." These two psychological states have been allowed to develop to the point that divorce seems inevitable. In such cases, any "cause" will do.

> The couple have . . . unconsciously created and seized on some justification for the split, a cause around which further to polarize and to escalate their war: his affair, her job, his mother—the issue itself matters little. The divorce process represents a hunger in both of them to be "born again," to leave behind a "sense of family" that denies their personhood. At last and at whatever cost they are determined to become two people.[2]

Dana F.'s experience was another case in point. At the time of her most severe marital stress, it seemed clear that her husband's impotence and general maladjustment to life were their primary problems. He was discharged from the army in a "force reduction" move, and he had had difficulty coping with this forced reentry into civilian life. He was a perfectionist, and both were very active in their church. Yet he began drinking heavily and refused counseling. Even though they qualified for service in their church's higher echelons, they were declared ineligible because of his problems. The last straw before their divorce was when both Dana and her husband had affairs.

It would be hard to compile a list of better reasons to divorce. Yet, looking back, Dana sees that a major part of their difficulty was the way she *reacted* to her husband's problems. For one thing, like Millie, Dana was trying to respond to her husband from a position of zero self-esteem. Even after the divorce she sought ways to reinforce her low opinion of herself. "I expended all my energies on activities to keep from looking inside myself," she says. "I didn't like myself so I bleached my hair."

Single again, Dana was raped twice. She explains that she didn't press charges because, "I felt I had brought all this on myself by my behavior," she says. Her "behavior" consisted of trying to look attractive; and without a good self-image she bought into the male-promoted myth that "a good-lookin' woman brings it on herself."

Now Dana believes it would have been better for her marriage, and *easier,* to work on problems such as self-esteem *before* the divorce. She regrets that she didn't have more patience with her husband's adjustment problems. "I wish I had communicated what I was really feeling and not been so wrapped up in what *I* wanted out of life with no regard for others," she says. "If I could do it over, I would find out what was causing my husband's impotence. I would be more demonstrative—freer at hugging and showing affection. I would have given it more time."

Dana speaks so poignantly of all this because a subsequent marriage lasted only six months. She realized too late that she had divorced before identifying the real enemy in her marriage.

Maybe She Isn't the Turkey

Not long ago a man in Turkey divorced his wife after a bitter, six-year court battle.[3] Their twenty-one-year marriage had been a mistake. They had nothing in common. Although it was a long, hard fight, the man was finally relieved of his problem wife. He was free.

Our Turkish friend then set out to find a replacement—

this time, the *ideal* spouse. To eliminate some of the guesswork, he went to a computer service, told them all about himself, and settled back to wait while the computers matched him with one of the agency's 2,000 prospective brides. Their selection? *The woman he had just divorced.* The divorce appearing to be a total failure, they remarried, with renewed commitment to be more tolerant of each other. Intolerance was the problem—not the spouse, not the marriage.

Author Delma Heyn tells of three women who looked back on their divorces with similar feelings. Sheila divorced her husband because she found him boring. Barbara left because her husband didn't want her to work. And Karen wanted out after her husband had an affair.

Now? Sheila looks back longingly at the serenity and security she had in her marriage. Barbara looks about her at the numbers of families in which both Mom and Dad work and believes if she had stuck it out, her husband would have changed. Besides, she now says, "What kind of jerk walks out on a husband simply to go to work?" And Karen, noting now that her husband's affair was short-lived, feels that they could have worked through it if she had stayed and they had sought counseling.[4]

All of these stories illustrate the wisdom of therapist Augustus Y. Napier, who notes that "the difficulties in marriage are not only between us but within each of us."[5]

It isn't easy to look within, to stop blaming others, or "the marriage," in the heat of a troubled relationship. But there are many rewards. In addition to possibly saving the marriage, you get to know yourself. To survive, you must accept yourself, warts and all. Then a wonderful new vista stretches out before you. Having accepted yourself, you often learn to accept your spouse, differences and all.

It was only because Jamie and Millie had the courage to ferret out the real problems within themselves that they could sit so relaxed and tell me of their lives today. They are still very different. At some points they have created practical ways to protect their differences. They have separate bank accounts to cut down on arguments about what to buy, agreeing that they will split expenses equally. They both have cars, so they can go when and where they please. But what they have in common is far weightier. Each has traits the other respects and needs.

And the kids all come to one home to celebrate Thanksgiving.

Twenty Times Worse

Unfortunately, a marriage counselor discouraged Dolores B. from discovering a similar truth about her twenty-three-year marriage in time to save it. Fortunately, she was intelligent enough to learn it herself in time to end a relationship that was about to lead to a new marriage—one that would have had many of the old problems.

"The last ten years of our marriage were just not what I wanted," Dolores explains. "So I sought that somewhere else. I'm a Christian, and had a lot of guilt, and went to counseling." It's not too surprising that her counselor had the well-worn modern aversion to letting anyone experience a little healthy guilt. But even if he thought adultery was OK, he should have taken Dolores' own experience of guilt seriously. Instead, she was encouraged to "go for it."

"He said my husband was hampering me emotionally," she said. "He said the children would bounce back and that I could make a new life." So she filed for divorce. But only two months after it was final, Dolores realized the mistake she had made. "I realized that I was just taking the same problems into a new relationship. I could see it all becoming twenty times worse than the twenty-three years with my husband, and I thought, *What have I thrown away? I'm looking at a house that I'm taking care of all by myself and two children that are hurting. My house is only half a home. . . . It's tough.*

But not as tough as it would have been had she remarried before meeting the enemy in herself.

CHAPTER SEVEN

Conflict Is a Growth Hormone

 confess—in the early years of my own marriage I thought that conflict was to be avoided at all cost (more on this in chapter 9, where I will tell how our own impending divorce failed gloriously). Gerry M. looks back on her marriage and sees the same tendency, particularly regarding her relationship with her mother-in-law.

Small—*Very* Small—Consolation

Gerry's husband Brian was still tied to his mother's apron strings. He was aggressive—even domineering—in other areas, but he could not stand up to his mother. Gerry argued regularly with Brian about it but was reluctant to speak with his mother about the problem. Finally, things came to a head during a typical argument about whether they would go to his family or hers for the Christmas holidays. Gerry and her parents were willing to have their Christmas on Christmas Eve, so Brian's family could host the couple Christmas Day—but that wasn't enough for his mom, who insisted they stay from the 23rd to the 25th.

"Well, Mother," Brian said in exasperation, "if it will make you happy I'll spend all that time with you, and

Gerry can go to her parents."

Said Gerry: "If we can have separate holidays, we can have separate lives." And they did. Of course since the divorce, their holidays are *very* separate.

But Gerry is still haunted by the woman. "I regret that I allowed a third person to interfere with my marriage," she laments. "Instead of confronting my mother-in-law early in the marriage myself, I expected Brian to handle the problem."

Of course Gerry was right to go to Brian first with the problem. His reluctance to confront his mother could be cited as the primary cause of the breakup of the marriage. But that's small consolation to Gerry now. Sitting alone at home, it's of little comfort to console herself that she was right. She now realizes that the marriage was worth confronting her mother-in-law.

Agitated Roots Grow Deeper

Gerry and Brian didn't allow the agitation of in-law conflict to serve as a "cultivator"—a plow that not only roots out weeds but also goads the roots of the plant we want to save into meeting the challenge of survival.

More than one couple has found that having the courage to confront can actually strengthen both their marriage and secondary relationships, including in-laws. In the first place daring to take a visible stand in favor of our primary relationships declares loyalty. It communicates to a spouse, "You are the most important person in my universe, and I don't want less important people to ruin what we have going for us."

In the second place, the courage to confront can declare boundaries to the in-laws, communicating to them, "You are important to me too—next to my own family. You can't run my family, but I do hope we can have cordial relationships as in-laws."

As author, professor, and marriage counselor Stuart Love writes:

Conflict is often the vehicle by which tension is relieved and frustrations are vented. Persons who have healthy doses of conflict are often less susceptible to the resentment that accompanies pent up anxieties and complaints. . . . Some might suggest that growth never occurs without the benefit of conflict in one form or another.[1]

Nice and Unattractive

Bonnie was a non-confronter too.[2] People are supposed to be nice, aren't they? Especially Christians. And especially women. Won't their husbands like them better if they don't rock the boat? The fact is, Frank interpreted Bonnie's "niceness" as a lack of personality strength and backbone. He found her dull and unexciting. That was only one factor in their divorce, but it was an important element.

Both Frank and Bonnie found that they could not forget each other. They found no one else as attractive. Also, Frank became a Christian and felt he should at least bury his angry feelings toward Bonnie. Maybe they could even be friends again. That was the beginning of the end of their divorce.

But remarrying an ex-spouse doesn't miraculously mend the relationship—as the couple proved one evening when they were telling their story at a seminar on reconciliation. When asked, "How are things going now that you are married?" Frank answered honestly, "Right at this moment, not the best. We had just a little bit of an argument coming up today."[3]

Why allow a couple still having trouble to be presenters at a marriage seminar? Because they have learned—especially Bonnie—that they don't have to allow arguments and disagreements to loom so large as to become a huge billboard spelling DOOM for the marriage. They had a remarkable plan: They would *discuss* their disagreement! And they would do it the very day it arose. They were now more honest about their feelings, and they took literally the biblical injunction, "Do not let the sun go down while you are still angry" (Eph. 4:26).

Letting Conflict Feed on Itself

Don't misunderstand. Handled the wrong way, conflict is anything but a growth hormone. Occasionally, you still hear of a marriage counselor using the language of the '60s and encouraging couples to "let it all hang out." You can still see reruns of the old Bob Newhart show, where he played a psychologist conducting group sessions in which everyone is given a pillow or soft "club." They flail away at each other, supposedly expending their anger in harmless "violence."

More recent research has concluded that it doesn't really work that way. Hitting, even in controlled circumstances, breeds a spirit of hitting. Couples whose pattern of conflict is merely a shouting match tend to achieve hoarse voices and hurt feelings more than conflict resolution. Destructive conflict feeds on itself, growing a monster that can devour any relationship.

The trick is to allow conflict to be *con*structive. This requires grit not to run away from it and also such elements as timing and finesse and ground rules. It demands the ability to put yourself in your spouse's place. It calls for negotiation and compromise. Feeding on itself under these conditions, conflict can become a cultivated plant instead of a wild and destructive weed. Changing the image, healthy conflict can become the abrasion in the oyster that produces a pearl.

Constructive conflict requires something of the same skill good writers use in revising their work. Many experienced writers speak of the difference between proofreading or editing a manuscript, and actually *revising* it. They point out that to revise means to "revision." The best "re-visioning" comes from leaving the manuscript for a few days, then coming back to it with a fresh outlook. "Revisioning" a manuscript requires more than putting the commas in better places. It requires stepping back and asking such questions as: How will that passage be taken by my prospective reader? Will the plot be better served if the character Josie first appears in chapter 2 instead of chapter 3?

As you can see, applying this skill to marital conflict could easily bring marriage partners to an angle of vision that enables them to see each other's point of view. If they allow it, this "revisioning" of each other can be something like the excitement of a first love. Part of the fun of courtship and dating is the fact that couples are on a quest to know and understand the mysterious depths of each other's souls. Quarreling couples could rediscover something of the excitement of the chase if they would allow "revisioning" to put their current relationship in a new and different light.

Fighting by the Same Rules

Unfortunately, some Christians believe that the husband is "the head of the wife" and that this gives him a built-in advantage in any conflict. That mistaken notion dooms many a fight before it starts. In Ephesians 5:21 Paul actually teaches that ideal Christian relationships are achieved by *mutual submission,* not male domination. Understanding this can help Christians model their style of argumentation after a scriptural pattern instead of after Archie Bunker—who settled his arguments with Edith by simply ordering her to "stifle it!"

In the case of Bonnie and Frank, mentioned earlier, Frank had to "revision" the rules by which he and Bonnie were fighting. Fortunately, he came to realize that the mere fact that he was a male and "head of the wife" did not give him the right to stifle Bonnie when she finally grew bold enough to state her feelings. Instead, he learned to be willing to hear her out and to state his own views, hoping for consensus.

In his book, *Love and Negotiate,* John Scanzoni outlines
useful "articles of war" for allowing marital conflicts to be
a source of growth instead of death. Each spouse must
grant that the other has the right to emerge from an argument with a need that is met: the hope is that both can
"win" in some way. Anger cannot lead to violence, or to
withdrawal (a favorite tactic of the male of the species).
Both parties must be open to a creative resolution of the
difficulty—one that had occurred to neither when the argument began.[4]

Scanzoni also makes the important point that not all
arguments can be resolved to both spouses' satisfaction.
He warns against the unrealistic expectation that total harmony must reign before a marriage can work.[5] As I point
out in chapter 9, that's a platonic view of marriage—if an
absolutely harmonious marriage exists anywhere, it must
be in an ideal world. Actually, it's like the city the Greeks
wrote about. It's Utopia, which means, literally, "nowhere."

Addicted to Conflict

For balance, a word of warning should be offered against
injecting yourself with the truth of this chapter so frequently that you become *addicted* to conflict. You've seen
the syndrome—a mother and daughter become so locked
into a pattern of disagreement and conflict that they carry
it into the daughter's adulthood, and they seem to *require*
an argument when they get together. Conflict has characterized their relationship so long that if they changed the
pattern, they would feel the other has stopped caring.

Psychologist Gerald May describes a similar addiction in
his own life. A few years ago he came face-to-face with the
realization that he habitually criticized people. He had become skilled at the rapier-sharp put-down, humiliating
people with the weapons of sarcasm and biting humor.
When he realized this about himself and tried to change,
he found that he was surprisingly locked in to his old
ways.

In trying to stop this behavior, I encountered all the struggles one might expect. I experienced withdrawal symptoms; I felt ill at ease when I didn't do it, and sometimes my anger came out in more direct and harsh ways. I had trouble facing the emptiness left by the removal of this behavior: "If I'm not going to crack a joke at this point, what *am* I going to do?"[6]

May reports some success in breaking this habit by prayer and meditation. But he confesses what many quarreling couples need to confess: the seeds of self-interest and insecurity are never far below the surface. In a marriage, conflict can seldom be constructive unless both spouses confront these subtle and addictive needs.

Author David Viscott muses wisely on this issue:

Is the price of living with another person always so steep? Do you always have to give up a part of yourself that you need? Is it going to be like this forever, wanting what you want but not being able to have it? Too many relationships are based on such childish, unrealistic ideas of possessing each other that it is difficult to grow and develop as an individual without hurting the other partner.[7]

Growth Can Also Be Uncomfortable

But what if each partner made the conscious decision to allow each other to grow *despite* the discomforts such growth can bring? The tragedy is that too many of us allow such inevitable discomfort to end the marriage before we test the stimulus conflict can provide for the growth of the relationship—as well as the individual.

Minister and author Harold Straughn notes that a couple's capacity for real empathy and caring *requires* conflict—even suffering—the kind of unfair treatment that ironically *ends* so many marriages.

Empathy is the result of having experienced a larger measure of suffering and injustice. No amount of information or reflection will suffice. Empathy is the prize we receive for bearing the burdens of responsibility, commitment, failure, and grief in behalf of a love relationship.[8]

Straughn maintains that this capacity to "bear one another's burdens" by accepting one of our own—and to grow from it—is a "Stage 5" marriage. His extremely perceptive book counsels couples to "divorce" immature stages of a relationship instead of each other—to hang on through what he sees as four passages that good marriages negotiate.

The fact is, if you leave a marriage because of conflict, you will probably enter a new relationship having no better conflict management skills than those that have brought you to the impasse in your present marriage. Odds are, the cycle will be repeated.

Of course, it's highly possible that divorce among us is so common not only because conflict has made the relationship painful, but also because we actually don't want to grow. That makes divorce doubly attractive: it promises relief from immediate pain and a change of environment that doesn't require the discomfort or effort of change and growth.

It's a little like discovering that Rytalin helped our preadolescent daughter's hyperactivity. Without it, she was high-strung, frequently in trouble, and tended to enter a room by ricocheting off the walls. With it she was calm and well-behaved. But what self-respecting adolescent would rather be calm and well-behaved than ricochet off the walls? She managed to avoid regular doses of the medication because it threatened a lifestyle she liked.

So it is, undoubtedly, with some of our divorces. If conflict threatens to enable us to grow, we avoid both the conflict and the person whom we perceive to be causing it.

This is no Pollyannaish refusal to acknowledge the pain of a stormy relationship. It *is* a challenge to couples in such a relationship to ask whether it's as painful and nonproductive as divorce can be.

PART III

Stories of Short-circuited Divorces

There are plenty of explanations about why marriages fail. It's time to tell the stories of people who found that their divorces didn't work out so well, either. Sometimes going to the trouble of rebuilding a relationship is a lot less trouble than ending it.

CHAPTER EIGHT

Fortunate Failures—Divorces Shattered by Remarriage

t should be obvious by now that the purpose of this book is not to recommend that everyone who regrets divorcing should remarry the ex-spouse. Some exes have married another person. Even if both are still single, the problems which caused the divorce may not be subject to change. As one tearful woman told me, "I would remarry him in a minute if he weren't still an alcoholic." That is a huge "if."

Stories of people who *have* been able to remarry each other, after their divorce failed to bring the happiness they sought, can worsen the pain of those who wish for a similar reunion. Yet I am going to risk this possibility and tell two such stories. They will encourage some for whom remarrying their ex-spouse is still possible. The fact is, these accounts contain too much hard-won experience and too much joy to go untold. They are presented here to show that in some cases the anguish of divorce has been transformed into the happiness of reunion.

Jay and Marsha

So many in our culture treat breaking up a marriage about as seriously as running a red light. But there are a few people, like Jay, whose attachment to family seems to be part of the structure of his soul. For him breaking up family is like pulling his heart out by the roots. For such people, divorce often fails.

The End of the Beginning

Jay is a pastoral counselor. Naturally, he is called on to work with women as well as men, often concerning intimate issues; but Jay's wife Marsha could not treat this "naturally."

"My wife was very jealous of me and all my relationships with women," Jay recalls, "especially if I seemed at all attracted to them." It was a tension that seemed to form the backdrop even to happy scenes in their life.

Early in their marriage the couple had dabbled in pornography, which proved to be a mistake that haunted them. It was confined to the privacy of their bedroom, and at first Jay thought it could only enhance their sexual relationship.

Unfortunately, Marsha had a history of sexual abuse which allowed the porn to take on a sinister dimension. Its illicitness reminded her of secret, shameful sexual experiences. Although they stopped using the pornography, it had apparently been the occasion for Marsha to project many of her confused sexual feelings onto Jay. Four long years later she was still angry at him for having brought the salacious material into their bedroom.

Her feelings for Jay became increasingly ambivalent. "She seemed to love me one minute and then hate me the next, for no apparent reason," he says. Obviously they needed outside counseling. (Despite their counseling skills, it's often impossible for professionals to "use them on" their own family. Even if they are able to be objective, family members expect from them love—with all its subjectivity.

But Jay felt that it was mainly Marsha who needed "fixing," and she did not really seem serious about counseling. Also, her mood swings kept him off balance. Even when she was seemingly in a good mood, he did not trust it to last. Weekdays were barely bearable because he was at work much of the time; on weekends they would fight.

Eventually, Jay realized they were destroying each other. But "the last nail in the coffin," as he puts it, was put in place when his friendship with a woman at his counseling office exploded into a romance. He and Marsha separated, then divorced. The children stayed with her.

Haunted by Tearful Dreams

Jay had not anticipated how deeply rooted his sense of family was. Seven months after the divorce he still found himself dreaming about the good times with his wife and children and waking up in tears. "There were days I could not even enjoy visiting my children because I cried the whole time," he recalls. "Every time I dropped the kids off at the house my little four-year-old son would stand at the window and wave until I was completely out of sight. My tears made it difficult to drive.

"I lived in fear that Marsha would remarry, and that my children would be raised by another man who might not love them, and who might move 'my' family to another state. I never got over the feeling that they were still my family, and that I belonged with all of them."

Eventually, Jay's basic honesty forced him to face his own role in the breakup of his marriage. From blaming his wife he moved into a state of being consumed with guilt for his extramarital fling. Although his counseling practice was church-related, he found no solace there. "Church people would come up to me and solemnly tell me, 'God hates divorce.' I finally began to snap back, 'God doesn't hate it nearly as much as I do because He never had one.' People would have been more helpful if they had just listened. By the time a divorce occurs, sermons don't do anything but drive you away from the church."

Jay tried to assuage his guilt by doing little things for his family from a distance, helping in the small crises that accompany child rearing. He took long walks trying to still the storm in his soul. Music sometimes helped, he says, although listening to hymns was too painful. Sometimes, during the congregational singing at church, he would be overcome with emotion and have to leave.

Unfortunately, Marsha did marry someone else. But she carried into the new relationship some of the problems she had experienced in her first marriage, and her second relationship failed too.

Against All Odds

With both of them shaken by the internal and external chaos in their lives, Marsha and Jay took a second, long look at each other. They could not shake the sense that they and the children were *family,* and that they needed to be family to each other. Yet, with his training and experience in counseling, Jay knew that nothing short of a miracle would enable them to get back together. Marsha's remarriage had indicated to him that she was still a very dependent person. Unless both of them could renegotiate their marriage on more independent terms, it was foolish to think of a reconciliation.

But the miracle happened.

Marsha began to work on a very independent relationship—one with God, which did not depend on Jay as a kind of priest. Suddenly, she appeared to Jay in a new light. She was no longer exerting pressure on him to be both her husband and a go-between with God.

Meanwhile, Jay's relationship with his new girlfriend was suffering a fortunate failure. Although he had learned that divorce "can make you very serious about changing yourself instead of your spouse," he was unable to rid himself of a certain resentment toward his girlfriend for her own role in "this whole nightmarish mess." They soon realized that they had no basis for a lasting relationship, and they broke up.

Five days later—and five years after their divorce—Marsha and Jay were reunited. They asked each other for forgiveness and prayed together that God would forgive them also. Soon they remarried and moved to another city to start over. Now, three years later, Jay beams as he says simply that "we are very, very happy."

Jay's Advice Now

Today Jay has a new tool for his work as a counselor, one which cost him dearly, but one he learned how to use in the crucible of experience. The tool is this: the understanding that few people with any sense of devotion to family can actually anticipate the pain of breaking it up.

He also advises: "If you divorce, stay single. If you can't stay single forever, at least wait several years before marrying again." The fact is, as Jay discovered, "it is practically impossible to start a new relationship before the other one is completely dead." In his case, "I found it impossible to deepen the new relationship, and it severely complicated and prolonged my grief-work for my ex-spouse."

Jay continues, "No one tells you how bad divorce really is, and [even after having experienced it] I can't even adequately describe it. Most of the silly little self-improvement books talk about what a positive, courageous step it can be." Referring to such books, he explains, "They're a bunch of baloney."

Both from his own experience and from his training, Jay simply asserts that "divorce is nearly always a crippling event for both spouses and for all the children involved."

An exception also grows out of his experience: When the trouble involves alcoholism, "Divorce is usually the only way."

But in almost every other case, he says, "If you will spend one-third of the time, money, adjustment, and effort you have devoted to the divorce working on the marriage instead, you'll usually stay married.

"Divorce is a monkey-trap," he concludes, a way out of

a painful situation "that looks great until the door springs shut behind you."

The Adamsons: A Family Again

I was sitting across from Carl and Katie Adamson, the minister and his wife from whom you heard in chapters 2 and 3. They are the picture of the ideal couple. Nothing in Katie's eyes or in Carl's gentle, pastoral manner betrayed the fact that they had only recently gone through a separation that failed—failed, that is, to prove permanent. Like my own marriage (see chapter 9), the Adamsons' march toward the divorce court was interrupted. "How did it happen?" I wondered aloud.

Katie, red-haired, slender and open, began. "I guess we were what everyone thought was the ideal couple—madly in love, perfect family, two kids and one on the way. I would never have believed we'd have problems.

"But I woke up one morning and found out that my husband's feelings were gone. That was a shocker for me, and it took me an extremely long time to believe it, to understand it, and to admit it. Of course, as a pastor's family we were in a fishbowl, and people were always telling us what a lovely family we were. It made reality harder to see. We went into marriage knowing something of how it would be, but we couldn't realize the power it would have over us."

No Leaving or Cleaving

Part of the hard reality that was causing problems in the Adamsons' marriage was Katie's inability to make the break from her parents and establish an autonomous home of her own.

"One of my big problems that I discovered later was leaving my family and 'cleaving' to my husband," she admits. "We were a long way from home. It was the first time I'd lived away from my family.

"We had had a huge fight even before we married, during some premarital counseling. We were taking a test and preparing our answers, and we compared them before going back to see the minister—which you're not supposed to do—and we were just totally opposite on this point. He'd say, 'Who are you talking about here?' and I'd answer, 'My family.' And he would say, 'But *I'm* your family!' I didn't catch the significance of that at the time."

Katie had especially idealized her father although not without ambivalence. "My father was a workaholic and didn't spend a lot of time with the family. And in turn, I tried hard to earn the kind of relationship I wanted with him but couldn't have. So he was on a pedestal. But shortly before our own problems came to a head, my dad fell off the pedestal. I simply didn't have the tools, the wherewithal, to deal with all of that and our own family situation too."

So with problems on two home fronts, modern couples talk it out and/or get counseling, right? It's not that simple for a minister and his family. They were in a small town, where word would have spread rapidly had they gone for counseling. The Adamsons felt that it would damage their credibility and their ability to minister. That meant: "Stuff it." Furthermore, Katie's home had not prepared her for marital conflicts.

"Conflict resolution in my own family hadn't really given me the background for conflict in marriage," she said. "My dad was always right. He'd listen to my mom, but then he'd say how things were going to be and that was it. He always won."

Like Father, Like Son (-in-Law)

Katie's father wasn't just a workaholic at "work." As he grew financially able to spend less time at his business, he devoted more and more of his time to lay tasks for the church. Suddenly Katie found that "being right" and being overly busy in "the Lord's work" characterized both her father, who had fallen from his pedestal, and her husband. It was a connection that had devastating effects.

For Carl's part, the demands of ministry made it impossible, he felt, to devote a great deal of time to his marriage. "The work of the church had to go on," he recalls. "Just because these marital problems were going on didn't mean I could stop doing what I was supposed to do. I was involved, of course, in marriage counseling while my own marriage was falling apart. I was in a sink-or-swim situation with the church, which had been desperately hurt by the previous pastor. The actual membership had gone way down. And frankly, it was a stepping stone. I felt that if I were going to have any future at all, I was going to have to do a really good job at this church. Almost from the first day, I was working my way out of there and I really took my work seriously. I worked very hard.

"It was like I was living my life in two spheres—there was the church and there was our marriage. We weren't really there for each other. We had been feeding the congregation's expectations without taking care of our marriage. And of course things dried up in bed, and there wasn't a lot of affection."

"We hadn't really learned how to be intimate," Katie explained. Somehow, as a minister's wife, she felt inhibited. "Even with my friends, I never felt I was really 'me.' It wasn't that I had deep, dark feelings to hide. But it was a long time before I finally just unpeeled myself to a friend, and that was a lot of relief."

Meanwhile, however, there was no relief in the communication block between them. Carl explained, "Finally, as the conflict really entered our relationship, we simply locked horns and butted heads, and we weren't really able to break through. It just happened time and time again. And with that, came the frustration. The conflict itself is one thing. But to pile the frustration on to the conflict, then you have blow-ups and explosions—and that's what we ended up having. It was such a negative environment."

"We went a long time," Katie said, "without letting anybody know what was going on. We kept smiling and kept being 'the perfect family.' " She accused Carl of allowing his church duties to interfere with his ability to deal with the family problems.

Carl says he would try to explain, " 'Look—it's my *job,* it's my bread and butter. If we *don't* do this, I'm going to be out of a job. We have got to keep our lives to ourselves. We cannot dump it all out on the whole church because I've got to bring home the bacon.' Katie thought that was just feeding my fat ego. This is an example of the way we communicated. Her perspective of things and my perspective were so very different that we just missed each other."

What to do? It would make sense to talk things out with Dad; so Katie's parents planned a visit. Unfortunately, they canceled the trip because—of course—her father was too busy at a new church. So busy, in fact, that he failed to call his daughter for a two-month period—a very crucial time for Katie.

From a Ripple to a Tidal Wave

Carl explained the ripple effect this set up. "The church seemed more important to Katie's dad than she did, so she naturally had this growing resentment toward her father. And I feel like I got a lot of that. Because that's what she was hearing from me—that the church was more important than she was."

Feeling shut out of her husband's life, and carrying with her the conflict of loving and resenting her father—for similar reasons—Katie's ability to cope crumbled. "We fought it for about a year, in constant conflict," she recalls. "But we couldn't get past *Go.* It wasn't on a constructive level. It just caused more pain every time we talked."

As for Carl, "I had my coping structure all lined up. I had my buddies that I played racquetball with. They were both ministers, and outside the church, and that helped."

"But all my friends were in the church," his wife said, "and no matter where I went it wasn't safe to talk about it.

But I needed a friend too. I finally did go to someone and talk about it. Unfortunately, talking to her blew it wide open."

There seemed nothing to do but separate. And just when things between them had built up to the flash point, Katie's father finally made contact. When he learned of her stress, he offered Katie a job if she would come "home" — a significant way of wrongly defining the word. She accepted.

"Was the separation, in your mind, headed toward divorce?" I asked. "Or did you feel that it was in order for things to settle down so you could put your marriage back together?"

"In my mind we were headed for divorce," Katie answered. "Nothing was set definitely at that point, but that was our intention."

Carl agreed. "It was not a 'therapeutic' separation. We were headed for divorce."

Katie moved thousands of miles away to work for her father. For a time, Carl struggled to remain as pastor of his church. Eventually, however, two ministerial friends confronted him with his need to follow Katie in order to work on the marriage. Concerned also about how his marital problems would damage his leadership potential, Carl resigned. He moved close to where Katie now lived and secured a secular job.

Why Church-related Counseling Failed

Knowing the value of counseling from his own experience in the field, Carl wanted to give that resource one final chance, before divorcing. Did it help? "We had some good counseling, and some lousy," Katie said.

Carl picked up more on "lousy" than "good." At one point in the interview he said bluntly, "The counseling in my view didn't help." I asked him to explain, especially in light of his own counseling experience and ministerial view of marriage and divorce.

"Most counseling has as its goal the development of persons," he said. "I strongly believe that good marital counseling must have the goal of saving marriages. The development of persons will happen as a consequence of saving the marriage. But it's a tougher assignment than if you're saying, 'If you don't feel free, then get out.' I think that goal is a part of the lie that we've accepted from the secular world. The truth is that as we work on our covenantal relationships, we thereby honor something very deep within the person, and that is our own personal human dignity.

"Where is there dignity in simply walking out on a life-time commitment? Where is there dignity in just forsaking the most important promise you can make? We affirm our dignity by going to the wall for the covenant relationships we have in our lives. And I think the most critical of those is the marriage relationship. I believe that it's much healthier for persons to focus on saving, salvaging, developing, and encouraging the covenantal relationship of marriage. *That* builds personhood much more than simply sacrificing one's integrity by walking out on a lifetime commitment that's been made to another person. This sort of stuff that our culture portrays as 'true freedom'—just to break out of the shackles of a relationship and go find another—it just isn't true."

Carl believes individual counseling for marriage problems has more potential than joint sessions. "I think a lot of marriage counseling is damaging because you're in a place where you're encouraged to say whatever is on your mind, whatever you think. And when you're in a state like that, you're not thinking rationally. You say hurtful things that, yes, you're really thinking right then, but it does the other person absolutely no good to hear. It's not complete reality. You don't need to hide things, but there are some things you just don't say to another human being because they do nothing but cause harm.

"And I have often found that when you start talking about your feelings in a joint counseling situation, it really becomes a free-for-all. The counselor doesn't really see the truth of what's happening in those situations. You feel the need to make a case for yourself, and it's not necessarily the truth. In my experience, counseling has been overrated in the Christian community."

Where Is the Church?

What about the role of the church in all this?

Carl said frankly, "The church wasn't really that much help in our case. They really had no precedent for dealing with separated couples. They could deal with a divorce because they have a lot of precedent for that. And they could deal with families that don't break up or those that totally break up. But what they didn't have precedent for was families that were struggling but were separated and trying to get back together.

"In a sense the church can become almost a facilitator of divorce because it's taken the attitude that well, that's the way it is, and it hasn't dealt with it in a very theological manner. I know few pastors who have really done thorough exegesis of the biblical passages on divorce. It's basically, 'Well, these things happen.' Then the church has ordinarily kicked in *after* divorce in terms of divorce recovery work. But in terms of divorce intervention, the church has been really shy. The church has backed off. We haven't wanted to appear Catholic, in terms of our views on divorce. Neither have we wanted to appear rigid or legalistic.

"The church has sort of reacted against the excesses of the past, but in so doing, I think we've gone too far. And we've taken divorce as a part of life, rather than recognizing it as a scandal. Divorce *is* a scandal because it's clearly a violation of God's intention. It simply is not God's will. God's will is that we stay with marriage and make it work. Obviously, He doesn't want us to stay in a marriage in which we're abused, but even that doesn't make an *ipso facto,* slam-dunk case for divorce. I don't think that ulti-

ALDI

Store #73

940 Quincy Ave, Ottumwa, IA

Visit us at www.ALDI.us

Your cashier today was Liz

Strawberries	0.99	F1
SUBTOTAL	0.99	
0.99 1-Taxable @0.00%	0.00	
AMOUNT DUE	0.99	
T O T A L	**0.99**	
1 ITEMS		
Cash	0.99	

*4391 0073/002/109   05/21/12 12:13pm A00

****

More Summer. More Savings.

Thank you for shopping at ALDI.

mately there is ever a *justification* for divorce. There are explanations; there are excuses, but I don't think we ever stand before God and explain the circumstances of our divorce and God says, "Well, in your case, OK. . . . "

A Sense of Family

I could see that Carl's convictions about the sanctity of marriage ran deep, and that this was part of the reason he had pursued Katie and tried to work on the relationship, even in their separation. What else was at work?

Carl answered. "First of all, I'm a family man. I don't have a night out with the guys for poker or play golf. I have strong male relationships, but my favorite role is as a husband and father—I'm just a family man. So when the separation occurred, I moved Katie back to her family, and I got an apartment in the same area so I could at least be near the kids.

"One day I woke up and said, 'What am I doing in an apartment without my kids?' I didn't want to be single. That was one part of it, just the discomfort of life as it was. I knew that it was just not 'me.' "

Katie agreed. "Carl never was the kind of father you read about in these cases who would not spend time with the kids. He truly wanted to be with the kids.

"And having the kids all the time—that was hard for me. All the things you read about the difficulty single moms have—it's a lot of pressure, and that added to the conflict. You just don't have anything left over after a day's work, and you can't give them what they need."

"Saving the family was the entrée into saving the marriage," Carl continued. "When you've got kids, you've got a very special trust. It's no longer just the two of you. Now there's a family. There was that entrée and those reasons for hanging on, for delaying—we had these precious children entrusted to our care." (You may want to reread what the Adamsons had to say regarding children and divorce in chapter 3.)

A Stolen Look at Love

One day Carl went over to Katie's house. "She wasn't there, but I had a key for when I visited the kids. So I went in and here was Katie's diary. I started going through her diary, and I couldn't believe the expressions of love. So I called her on the phone, and I told her I'd looked at her diary and how much it moved me. I tried to initiate something we could do together. But that evening when we were together, all my fears returned. Nothing had changed, and I was just feeling this mountain of frustration. So I backed off. I just went into a mode of visiting the kids as much as I could. That went on for about six weeks, with some intermittent conflict mixed in with it."

"Intermittent *major* conflict!" Katie added.

"That's right. And I couldn't keep the kids at the place I was staying, so when I had them, I had to rent something else. You know, 'This week I'm the Disneyland Dad'—that sort of thing. But we had this going on for almost two whole years.

"I finally decided we should try to just find times when we could be together and not deal with our differences, when we would just try to have some positive times. The weekend of my birthday that year we went out on a fairly ordinary family outing. I bought a bed for the girls—their apartment was so small that we got a daybed to conserve space. And it was just a positive time. And another time we went to the mountains together."

"We were trying," said Katie. "There was just too much pain to keep getting into it. And I was scared to risk too much because the arguments would threaten what coping ability I'd been able to gain back, so I was very cautious and very protective when we were together. The first month [of Carl's attempts to have positive times together] we spent almost all our free time together—weekends and whatever—and it was all centered around the kids. We avoided being alone. We avoided talking about the issues. I think this allowed for some healing, and it gave us back some of the family life we had lost.

A Break and a Breakthrough

Meanwhile, Katie's new work situation set her up for the kind of break she needed to make from her family of origin. "God put me in a place where I had to be with my dad day in and day out," she explains. "I had to deal with some of the issues between us. I had to stand up to him. I had to tell him I had to make some of my own decisions, instead of trying to do what he wanted me to do. And I think I was able to finally see the things in my family that were dysfunctional, and how far back they went.

"I also saw my sister, whose second marriage was falling apart, and she could no longer just blame the person she was living with, so she was feeling some of the similar family things I was. I found an ally in her, and we were able to talk about what had really gone on in our family life. We could say, 'Do you remember this?' and 'Was Dad like this to you?' And all that was very therapeutic for me."

Finally, Katie revealed something of what she had learned to Carl. "We were having Christmas together," Carl recalls, "again because of the family—and Katie made a statement that created the breakthrough, the opening I had been looking for. She said that she had finally come to realize that she had grown up in a dysfunctional family. And I thought, *Well, finally! She's discovered that her family members aren't perfect.*

"Earlier, when I would try to talk with her about her family, she would come back at me and attack my family. And, of course, my family has their problems too. But that wasn't the point. She was taking what I said as an attack on her family and as my contending that my family is perfect. But I viewed it as just a statement of reality that she needed to deal with. And her family was interfering. They were interfering in our relationship, with our kids, with my career. When she finally said that she realized some of this, it said to me that she was finally beginning to 'leave' her family and strike out on her own.

"And of course I had to admire her for that, and for the way she was managing in general. She was in the position of being a single mom, and she was doing a great job with the kids, holding things together, maintaining a home, and she exhibited a toughness that I don't think she thought she had, and I admired that.

"Just before we had this breakthrough, I'd taken the family car and put brakes on it and had some transmission work done. I wanted to make sure she was in a safe situation with the kids, and I wanted to show that I admired what she was doing. It was important to me — the sign that she was leaving her family — that's such a fundamental piece of marriage."

With that fundamental breakthrough, Carl and Katie's impending divorce was doomed. It wasn't just that Katie learned that her family of origin wasn't perfect. It was also that she realized that imperfections exist in all families, and that only by "leaving and cleaving" could she put herself in a position to work more objectively on the dysfunctional elements in her own marriage.

After a few more months, during which Carl and Katie began to enjoy each other's company again while not airing their problems, and then to discuss their problems with more mutual understanding, they reunited. The love they had known, but that had been diluted by the haunting presence of Katie's previous family, grew to the extent that they once again were able to take up the demands of ministry. Now they are with a large church where they serve effectively, especially in areas that strengthen families.

Lessons Looking Back

What have the Adamsons learned through their struggle that might help others in similar situations?

"Actually, we failed miserably on our own," Carl says. He believes that only when he and Katie stopped trying to "fix" things from their own points of view was God's own enabling grace able to come through. "We tried everything to work it out ourselves, but ultimately we both really felt that it was God's grace that put our marriage back together. It was only when we said, 'God, I'm sorry. I can't work on it anymore,' and just tried to be a family again, that things worked out.

"And of course the main lesson from our story is that the first command of marriage is . . . "

"Is one of the hardest!" Katie interrupted.

"Right," said her husband, with an understanding grin. "But the first command is "to leave," and then the second commandment is "to cleave," to cling to your spouse."

"And I see so many people getting married who are just like I was," Katie said. "I didn't understand about 'leaving your father and mother.' "

"And with her admitting this thing about her family, I could drop my attack," Carl added, "although I didn't mean it as an attack. But now I could simply make observations, and they were no longer viewed as attacks on her family.

"And incidentally, I think her family has grown in all of this. Before, they treated me as they treated two other sons-in-law that had divorced out of the family. And that was to communicate that I was the worst imaginable person. I was sick, I was this, I was that."

"And to this day, I don't think they did this maliciously," Katie said. "It was to protect their daughter."

That made sense to me out of our own family experience, so I asked: "And was what they were doing just an extension of the general style of family interaction in the home, rather than a personal attack on a son-in-law as such?"

"That's right," Carl agreed. "And that style is—don't ever let on that anything's wrong in public. You present yourself as though you're just the closest family imaginable. There would even be these very intimate statements of love to one another when an audience was present. But at home none of that intimacy was there. It was all a public presentation of the family.

"And my family context had been just the opposite. Any intimate statements about our love or the way we felt about one another happened when there was just family around. If there were spectators, we just wouldn't use that as an opportunity to make statements of love and appreciation for each other."

We've noted in chapter 2 what Carl and Katie learned about how expensive divorce is. Of course, since their planned divorce failed, they look at it positively. As Carl put it, "From one standpoint we 'bought' an intact marriage with our investment." He thinks the $12,000 it cost them even to put the marriage back together isn't bad "tuition" to learn how wrong divorce was for them. "And the diploma we got for it is an intact marriage license," he says.

"Also, we both believed in prayer before, but we really believe in prayer now," Carl says. "Those kinds of experiences really taught us dependence upon Christ. Our adequacy to ruin a marriage and our inadequacy to save it— these kinds of expensive lessons are what we purchased with that investment."

In Carl and Katie's new ministry together, they have been frank to speak of the struggle in their marriage. "When I preached on divorce," he said, "I told the whole congregation that as a pastor I wasn't speaking from isolation, that we had been through 'a season of difficulty' for two years—that I had been out of the church because of problems like this that came our way.

"Anyone who was asleep didn't sleep much after that. It had the positive effect of putting Christ on the pedestal instead of the minister, if anyone had him there. At the same time, as a pastor you want to be in an exemplary posture. It's an ongoing balancing act."

CHAPTER NINE

How Our Planned Divorce Broke Up in Romance

 arly in this book I promised to relate in more detail how my own marriage survived an apparently inevitable divorce. Again, my wife Faye and I share our experience not because we're exemplary people for not divorcing, or even because easy "lessons" from our experience are transferable to others. The simple fact is that any marriage that survives the tensions on which most modern divorces are blamed can yield insights that are useful to others.

We were nothing if not thorough: we fought on all the classic battlegrounds of a troubled marriage—personality differences, power struggles, sex, finances, child rearing, in-laws, and religion. We had several separations, and I was personally convinced that divorce was inevitable. But here's how we discovered that it's a myth to assume that these classical clashes must end a marriage.

The Trouble with Heaven

I grew up with a view of marriage that was so heavenly minded it was of no earthly good. Years later, when I studied philosophy, I learned that this was partly because I'm a "platonist" at heart. I was enthralled with Plato's

fascination for "ideals," the good, the beautiful, the true —
in other words, *perfection.* Of course, I wanted the ideal
marriage. And for me that meant no real arguments, no
conflict, just a static state of perfection. This unrealistic
expectation ill equipped me for the wear and tear of normal human relationships.

In my boyhood home, I never heard my parents argue
seriously. As I grew old enough to engage in serious Bible
study, I was impressed with the possibility of finding an
ideal way . . . a way back from the Fall to ideal harmony.
For human relationships I loved the Old Testament passage: "Can two walk together, except they be agreed?"
(Amos 3:3, KJV)

And sure enough, I found a young lady during my senior
year of high school who seemed ideal for just such an
agreeable "walk." The gossip column in the school news-
paper dubbed us a natural match. After "going together,"
as we said then, for nearly three years, we agreed that we
were a heavenly match too. Although we disagreed over
religion at some points, we were from similar backgrounds, agreed on basic values, and hated to argue. I
agreed to join Faye's church, we agreed to marry, and Faye
agreeably quit school to work in order for me to finish
school.

The amazing thing about our story is that all this agree-
ability stood out as a major feature, to others, for some
twenty years. Of course we had some disagreements — especially over finances, and how to raise the four boys and
adopted daughter who eventually blessed our home. But
each such ripple in the marital waters made us seasick; so
we quickly poured oil on it, or tried to forget about it. The
overall harmony endured through job changes, from
teaching school to journalism to the ministry. It remained
a dominant feature through the strain of adjusting to life
in an overseas mission. The pressure of feeling that a minister's family should be a model for the world added to the
unstated motto on our family crest: peace at any price.

The trouble with heaven is that too many of us perfectionists assume we can create it on earth. Whether or not a marriage is "made in heaven," it is called on to endure this-worldly strains and stresses. Real relationships aren't an ideal, static state, but an earthly *process.*

The outwardly smooth surface of our relationship was not a process at all. It was a fixed dam, holding back a flood.

The first crack in the dam occurred during our mission in the land "down under."

My Theological Change of Life

One of the less admirable items which I carried halfway around the world and checked through customs in Australia was a simplistic and legalistic brand of Christian faith. It was long on the necessity of duplicating all the relevant patterns and commands I could find in Scripture; but it was short of the freedom and joy of the Gospel. And it was an exclusivist brand of faith, questioning the salvation of everyone who didn't agree with my brand.

One morning I found myself in the lovely city of Canberra, the nation's capital, for an evangelistic campaign in which I was supposed to share my relatively joyless, but *certain,* message. Unfortunately, I had been nursing certain *un*certainties not only about my sectarian interpretation of the Good News but also about faith itself. Looking back on it, after dealing with myself and others who were entering midlife, I think I was going through a kind of theological menopause.

My sleep was troubled and fleeting, and I arose early. Looking out over the red-tiled roofs of Canberra, I visualized the generally happy-go-lucky, if thoroughly secular, Aussie families gathering for "brekka" (breakfast). Why should I presume to interrupt such scenes with a cheerless list of religious duties. With such a contorted view of my mission and ministry, I was suddenly overwhelmed with a realization that made my palms go clammy: *I have no message for these people.*

I was panic-stricken. The bags in which I had been carrying my religiosity had suddenly developed holes, and my faith threatened to leak out. Cutting my stay in Canberra short, I fled back to Sydney, desperate to unpack my theological baggage for Faye to wash. At least I expected her to be as jolted as I was by the stark clarity of my questions. Of course I was disappointed. No one could fully share the agony of my questions since they were as much the result of emotional unrest as rational doubts.

In that strange alchemy that enables us to transform fear into anger, I blamed Faye for much of my plight. After all, hadn't I joined "her church"? As I began to share some of what I was feeling, it was Faye's turn to panic. Here she was 8,000 miles from home, with five kids and a husband apparently losing his faith or his mind, or both—and saying that she was somehow responsible. The terror in her eyes, and our previous emphasis on total harmony, enabled me to commit a *felix culpa*—a "fortunate sin." I stopped the blaming process, which was fortunate at the moment; but it was unfortunate that I feared that even expressing how I was feeling would lead to the kind of argument our self-enforced serenity did not allow.

I simply needed a break from the religion game, I told myself. We returned to the States, and I found an accepting fellowship of Christians where I could safely air my doubts. My theological crisis was eased when I was able to get work again as a journalist. We concentrated on raising children—and seeking tranquility as the common denominator of our marriage.

My Search for Mother

The time away from the ministry proved to be a time of healing for my theological wounds. After additional training in pastoral counseling, I reentered the ministry. The training gave me new self-confidence, and the realization that our marriage had been too placid for its own health. Faye and I had misunderstood the peculiar arithmetic of marriage to mean something like "two halves make a whole." Finally, I realized that in marriage "one plus one equals one"—one whole person plus another whole person equals one healthy marriage.

At least I understood the formula intellectually. What I didn't understand was that I had never outgrown my desperate, childlike need for "mother"—the unconditional acceptance of a woman. Predictably, I handed to Faye this need that was left over from my experience as an adopted child. In my midlife immaturity, I reasoned that since my wife did not accept my theology, approach to child rearing, financial priorities, or my enjoyment of a glass of wine, she did not accept *me*.

There seemed to be nothing to do but to separate—and probably to divorce. First, however, I would oblige Faye by going to counseling—certain that this would help her see that divorce was objectively right for us.

Midlife Mayhem

Fortunately, one "objective" fact counseling and reading provided me was that part of what I was feeling was related as much to my age and stage as to my marriage. Unfortunately, I found that I was engaging in a favorite midlife pastime—dredging up the past and examining it in its worst light. In my case, it was a scene right out of the comic strip "Bloom County." It was as though some menopausal hormone as potent as those surging through Bloom County's adolescent hero made me open the door to the dark closet of the past. Inside were shadowy shapes and raucous voices claiming that I'd neglected them and clamoring for attention. As vicious as they were, they had a certain appeal because they claimed I had been wronged, that my point of view had been summarily dismissed. My "civil rights" in marriage had been treated uncivilly. Differences between Faye and me that were once manageable now seemed intolerable. They were no longer simple disagreements; they were sure signs of rejection. Midlife sensitivities made us both so fragile that we each needed more affirmation than either could give.

Much has been written since those years on "male menopause" and midlife crisis. Rather than summarize that material, let me give a personal perspective of what my marriage felt like at midlife.

The single most vivid sensation, for me, was panic. Amid all the other typical symptoms — vocational crisis, decline in sexual potency, the feeling of running out of time — the most dominating factor was the urge to cut and run. Researchers still do not agree whether midlife brings to males an actual change in body chemistry. But for me it *felt* like the hormonal riots of adolescence, or the stress reaction in which adrenaline is dumped into the bloodstream, producing the well-known fight or flight response. A generally nonassertive person, I could only flee.

The world — and especially my marriage — seemed to be closing in. The sensation of smothering sometimes made it physically hard to catch my breath. I had palpitations of the heart and other classic physical symptoms of anxiety attacks. I had to have air. More than once I fled to spend the night alone at a nearby lake. I was unable to maintain my ministry, and I fled that post too. Fortunately, I found a writing job in a nearby city, and when I escaped to that new work, I informed Faye that this time my departure was to be considered a separation. Although I had once prided myself on being steady and stable, I now strove in vain to curb the pattern of panic and flight.

With our relational problems complicated by such visceral forces, surely the merely cerebral work of counseling or the power of moral obligation could not possibly save us from divorce. But another more positive thing was happening. Our unstated but firm agreement not to disagree openly was being undermined by slow progress in negotiating skills and learning to "fight fair" — openly, in a clearly marked arena, and above the belt.

But there was one huge obstacle both of us were reluctant to face: the romance had faded from our marriage.

When the Feeling Is Gone

During one of our heated sessions Faye blurted out the question all quarreling couples face, but which they cannot always bring themselves to ask in their raw and tender state. It is often stated in terms of "Don't you love me anymore?" In Faye's case, it came out, "Would you marry me if we had it to do over again?"

As we talked, it became apparent that bound up in that question was the fear that the feeling had never been genuine, else it would not appear now to be gone.

I had good news and bad news. The feeling had been genuine; the feeling was gone.

Some Christian marriage guides belittle romantic feelings. It's too much to expect a marriage to retain them forever, we are told. Then we are treated to marvelous forays into the Greek language, designed to show how unimportant romantic feelings are over the long haul. Really good marriages, we are told, have *agape*—the kind of love God has for us, a rational decision to love despite the actions of the beloved. This is supposed to be far superior to *eros,* the mere romantic attraction between human lovers, and to *philos,* the love of friends. When we rise to the heights of *agape,* we act in loving ways, whether the feeling is there or not.

Certainly it is true that romantic feelings change from the first tingly rush many people feel upon "falling in love." We do need a concept of love strong enough to keep covenant with a lover beyond the mood of the moment and past the beloved's occasional unloving acts. Author Dalma Heyn recently quoted "Sheila," who looked back with regret on her hasty divorce and said wistfully:

> No matter how much you want to believe that marriage is an extended love affair, it just isn't. No woman in the world is in a perpetual state of adoration and excitement over a man she's with for years and years.[1]

But the alternative to a "perpetual state of adoration and excitement" is hardly the absolute disappearance of *eros*. Thousands of long-term marriages accept the natural decline of the "tingle" or the perpetual state of excitement but replace it with a less intense feeling of romance that is a burning all its own, a fire that is all the more lasting for its relatively lower flame.

And while I am thankful that God loves me *agape*-style, people are only human, and we need the other forms of love. Even after thirty years of marriage, Faye and I still required *eros* and the warm fuzzies of romantic attraction. We wanted to smooch with the person to whom we were married. We needed to hear something more than a lofty announcement that "in spite of your faults, I have made a rational decision to love you anyway." It isn't a sin to be human; and the very human perception of a partner's acceptance or rejection affects our ability to cuddle and coo.

So we had to face the fact that in all the conflict, the romantic feelings had faded. Both of us had changed too much to assume that we would have picked each other to marry if we had it all to do over again. Faye was exactly right when she cried accusingly, "You're not the man I married!" For one thing, I was much less sure of certain religious truths which she held to be essential in the man she married. For another, I had come to hold that change was the one essential sign of growth; I would have resented it if she had accused me of *not* changing. The stark fact was that at that tense moment neither of us would have walked down the aisle with the other to be bound in holy matrimony. Obviously, with the feeling gone, there was no choice but to divorce.

Or was there?

The Time of Our Lives

Looking back, it almost seems as though these problems consumed so much of our attention and emotional effort that we simply ran out of time to divorce. In another sense, the seemingly inevitable failed to materialize simply because we delayed it so long we lost interest. While these are not particularly lofty reasons for not divorcing, they underscore the importance of allowing time to do its work. But did we have that kind of time, at our age? Fortunately, my midlife feeling that I was running out of time was balanced by a long-standing need to analyze, to probe, to understand what goes on inside people, including myself. To Faye's eternal credit, she wanted to understand too, and she maintained a stubborn unwillingness to believe that we could not work things out. We both began to read the literature that was just beginning to be published on midlife crisis. We sought competent counseling. All this—fortunately—took time. And we learned that, clearly, we were caught up in a process which could be traumatic quite apart from our longstanding differences.

While I do not discount the inherent value of the counseling and the reading, I believe their primary value in our case was that the process bought us time. It was as though midlife trauma involves a buildup of "juices"—whether physical or mental—which time alone can drain away. The demons of midlife insecurity seemed to resist theological and psychological incantations. They required the steady erosion of gradual insight and the dissipating influence of sheer time.

I needed time to gain control over the panicky flight syndrome, to learn to stand my ground and "fight fair." It took time for Faye to realize that she projected, in the phrase of Transactional Analysis, a "strong controlling parent," and to cut me more slack. We both needed to conquer our inordinate need for total approval from each other. It took time for me to realize that I had an unrealistic view of marriage as an ideal haven instead of a ship strong enough to withstand the storm. If we could not make any headway on such issues, we would likely carry our handicaps into a new relationship.

One of our longer separations gave us time and space to relearn "individuation" skills—the subtle ability to be ourselves without its coming across as a violent emancipation proclamation. While we knew about this process in our children, we had not learned to apply it to our own relationship. One helpful step occurred when Faye had the courage to return to school and get her RN degree—after being a homemaker for thirty years and raising five children. This gave her more independence and self-respect, and in turn, increased my respect for her too.

It was also helpful when I joined another church. It was of untold value for us to realize that our marriage did not really depend on absolute religious uniformity. We developed different sets of friends. In time—and only in time—freeing each other in these ways freed us also to respect each other as a person in our own right, instead of a bookend which could not stand up without our rushing in as a prop.

We also needed to buy time in order to sort out our relational problems from many others which clouded the picture. Time allowed some of our differences in child rearing to dissipate as the last child graduated from home.

And there were the problems I was experiencing in my ministry. I had been a convert to "Faye's church." Suddenly it dawned on me that it had never become "my church." After years of ministry, I found myself questioning its basic doctrines and practices and resenting its demands. Because it was "her church," I found myself blaming Faye for my vocational crisis. Only with time could I realize that I was unfairly blaming her for decisions I had made. Only with time could I finally realize how foolish it would be to try to "fix" a theological problem with a divorce!

It took time for me to distinguish between real slights and midlife paranoia—to tell if my wife had actually behaved in a beastly way, denying me permission to be myself, or if the demons from the closet of the past were figments of my midlife imagination. Again, listen to "Sheila," who learned of this possibility too late: "What kind of jerk walks out on a husband simply to go to work? What kind of idiot seeks permission to live her own life? . . . I could have worked and been autonomous *and* married [emphasis mine] if I had not been so impressionable, in such a hurry. . . ."[2]

The modest amount of objectivity we were able to purchase with time helped us sort out other factors. We weighed the irritants we thought divorce would relieve against our need to parent our (grown) children jointly, and to grandparent theirs. We asked whether the financial blow of divorce would outweigh the stress we were experiencing in the relationship over finances. We tried to ask realistically whether being alone would be better than our abrasive togetherness.

We struggled, sometimes separately, sometimes together, for five years. Buying this much time isn't necessarily healthy. No one whose physical or mental health is really threatened by a marriage—especially when physical abuse, drugs, or alcohol are involved—should struggle as long as we did before divorcing. Also, there is little promise for a marriage if the protagonists simply become so exhausted that they surrender their points of view and lapse back into the relationship by default. But none of these elements were present in our case. We continued to maintain the right to our own viewpoint, while doing all we could to understand and accommodate that of the other.

I do think we instinctively felt that as long as we weren't killing each other *any* means of postponing the trauma of divorce was worthwhile. We intuitively projected ourselves into the painful reality described by author Pat Conroy after his own divorce:

> I have seen no one walk out of a divorce unmarked; it makes you a different person. You can enter the sinister cocoon as a butterfly and stagger out later as a caterpillar doomed to walk under the eye of the spider. . . . There are no laws of nature that apply—only laws of suffering, different for each individual.[3]

So our planned divorce failed. We were finally able to get back together *for good.*

And those feelings of love? Don't believe the myths about "You can't blow on dead embers and make a new fire." After first getting back together, the feelings were more like respect and appreciation for each other's willingness to struggle so mightily and to make positive attempts to change. Somehow, facing the fact that the old feelings were gone, freed us to ask what *new* feelings were possible. We treated the old romantic feelings as a gossamer-and-lace heirloom; we were sorry that our problems had made them go out of style, and it was necessary to accept some feelings of nostalgia as we packed them away in our memories. But we left the lid off; they lay as it were in a post-separation "hope chest." While not requiring them of each other, we didn't rule out the possibility that they might creep up on us unawares.

And, sure enough, it happened. It was something like night vision. Scientists say that because the center of our eyes lack the proper cells for seeing at night, we can actually see an object better by looking slightly to one side of it. In our case, we clung to each other with mutual permission not to have to "look" directly at romance. And lo! romance gradually emerged out of the darkness, eventually surprising us with a new intensity. We learned the wisdom of the common observation that feelings may follow behavior, not vice versa. Author Jo Coudert put it this way:

> It is one of those quirks of human nature that you love the person whom you treat well. . . . Love follows the trail blazed by generosity. . . . Thus, although it would seem at first glance that forbearance and patience and silence might exact almost too heavy a toll to bear, the opposite is true. The other will benefit, but it is you who will benefit greatly, for you will love more.[4]

But, of course, the appearance of love out of behavior is

a *process,* not an act; and, again, a process is a matter of time. We knew it was settling for second best to be content to warm ourselves by the embers of respect and appreciation, having known the joy of the more hotly burning flames of romance. But the coals were far better than the cold. And, finally, blowing gently on the coals created a draft which rekindled the flame. While the romantic feelings weren't "the same," they included such essential elements as sexual ecstasy—and there is nothing like ecstasy to overwhelm nostalgia for a version of romance that cannot be recreated.

So our experience is that it is mere fantasy to suppose that romance is impossible if you've changed so much that you have to admit that you wouldn't choose each other if you had it to do over again. Even if we had divorced and married someone more to our present choosing, this sort of courtship phase would have had to be negotiated. And if a new relationship would have to be nurtured from the dreamy haze of initial attraction to more mature romanticism, why not make that emotional investment in our own relationship?

To come full circle, there we were in the Bahamas for that second honeymoon. Romance? It rained every day, but it was not enough to dampen our ardor. We were like lovers who had stolen away for a secluded weekend. It allowed us to get better reacquainted.

And you can imagine how relieved we are today that we did not end our marriage because we were "going through a phase."

Phases pass. Marital needs last.

(By the way, although we found we didn't have to attend the same church to tend to each other in marriage, we began to grow together religiously more than ever until even that difference was overcome. We're now happily involved in a co-ministry.)

PART IV

Challenging the Myths about Divorce

Myths are dangerous not just because they aren't true, but because they contain half-truths. We wouldn't cling to them if they didn't speak to something real within us. Myths are dispelled only when we stare their reality down in the name of a stronger reality—something like the Gospel of Christ.

CHAPTER TEN

Five Myths about Divorce

s I said in the Introduction, I pray that these personal stories of divorces that failed will prompt people whose first thought is that divorce is a way to treat a troubled marriage to have second thoughts. These stories and the many others that could be told show clearly that the notion that divorce "fixes" things is a myth. In fact, some books dealing with the problem are bold enough to use the word—as in J. Allan Petersen's fine book, *The Myth of Greener Grass.*

Yet, as every marriage counselor knows, such books and stories alone cannot stem the tide of hasty divorces. Why? Because myths are often more powerful than actuality.

Why is this so? Doesn't Jack Webb of the old television show "Dragnet" speak for all modern people when he says he just wants the facts, ma'am? In our enlightened age, we're ruled by rational thought, not myth—right?

Wrong. Look at the following proof.

Myth over Matter

A folklore specialist in eastern Europe once researched the origins of a popular ballad of tragic love. It was "mythical" in the sense that it repeats themes found the world over—

themes of love found to be true everywhere in general but nowhere in particular.

The song tells of a spurned lover who is bewitched by a jealous fairy and thrown over a cliff. Shepherds find his body and bring it to the village for a funeral. There his bereft beloved sings a ballad of rustic beauty commemorating their tragic love.

Research turned up the surprising fact that the local version of these universal themes had actually grown out of a particular event. In fact, it had grown out of the actual experience of a woman who was still alive. Here was a fine opportunity to track down the facts of the case—to compare the myth with reality.

As you might guess, the woman's own version of the incident was quite different from the folksong. She had rejected her lover; he had slipped and fallen over a cliff; she had only repeated, along with other women at the funeral, the customary funeral liturgy.

So when confronted with the facts, people who loved the ballad immediately changed it, right? Wrong again. They insisted that time and grief had distorted the woman's memory. The true facts of the case had no chance at all against the more popular—and psychologically necessary—version. "It was the myth that told the truth: the real story was already only a falsification."[1]

Is "Romantic Love" Another Myth?

Another example, more directly related to marriage, is the "myth of romantic love." Experts have warned for years that the warm fuzzies of prenuptial days won't last forever. But anyone who has tried to tell this to a young couple head over heels in hormones, if not in love, knows that the power of the "myth" can overwhelm the facts.

Of course, all this should make us aware of the power of myth—of the fact that in some cases it is "truer" than the facts because it speaks to such a deeply rooted need. As long as we long for romance, it will do little good for researchers in white coats to tell us it doesn't exist. Furthermore, the fact that some people have "experienced the myth" — that is, been head-over-heels in love — means we can't just discount it.

Test Your Myth-Quotient

Harold Straughn lists several popular beliefs that make people of our day consider divorce. He calls them "a kind of popular folk-wisdom [that] has arisen in the absence of solid evidence."[2] That's not a bad definition of myth too. It might be enlightening to test your own acceptance of these popular measuring sticks that people in the grip of American marriage myths use to tell if their marriage is in serious trouble. *How true do these statements ring to you?*

- You no longer feel the same way about each other that you did when you first fell in love.

- You no longer enjoy doing the same things together.

- Your outside interests seem to be taking you in opposite directions.

- Your temperaments show no signs of becoming more compatible.

- Your values and attitudes have changed so much that the reasons you got married in the first place no longer apply.

- It's obvious your spouse isn't going to change, even though you've felt for a long time those changes would have to come.

- Your personal growth is more important to you

than ever before, yet your marriage is a hindrance, not a help.

● The children no longer depend on you the way they used to.

Chances are these popular symptoms of a marriage about ready to collapse have seeped into your mind regardless of your commitment to long-term marriage. If so, it's evidence again of the power of myth. It will be hard to convince with mere facts anyone who has bought into the culture's promise—however false—that divorce is a good cure for a bad marriage.

Stronger than Myth

How, then, can we keep from being ruled by unrealistic expectations? How can we dispel the power of myth? Only by recognizing that *the myth itself is a part of "the facts, ma'am."* It will do little good to write books against "the romantic myth," or against divorce, if we do not recognize that people cling to myths because they speak to something deeply true in their "innards," or put into words an in-depth longing or need.

Yet, however "real" myths are, as Christians we must affirm that we live by some rule more real than mere experience. Confessing that we live in a fallen world means that our "natural" experiences may not be *right*, even though they are *real*. To ignore such experiences, and the myths they engender, is unhealthy denial. But to submit to them without measuring them against the power of Christ would be to deny the Fall. And to deny the Fall is to make the fatal mistake of also denying that Jesus Christ came to redeem us from its effects.

The good news—the gospel—is that we can accept the myths, underlying power to speak to a genuine need, while also admitting their inadequacy. As powerful as these myths are, both the stories in this book and God's Word affirm that they are not the whole truth. As you read through the following myths, I invite you to confess both your humanity, to which they appeal, and the power of Christ to redeem you from their overwhelming power.

Five Myths about Divorce

1. "I'm So Lonely I Might As Well Be Alone."

The truth of this myth is the universal longing for companionship. It is the lived experience of the scriptural truth that "it is not good for man [or woman] to be alone." (See Gen. 2:18.) Someone once said that each of us is standing alone on the corner of a busy street, waving, and longing for *someone* to wave back.

But when a spouse doesn't "wave back," it's a sign to tend to the relationship, not to sever it. Everyone can learn to wave. No one — not your present spouse nor a future one — can wave all the time in precisely the way you need in order to feel connected.

And as several of the interviews in this book have revealed, being *relatively* alone in a marriage can be far better than being *absolutely* alone. Before you divorce, remember a time when your parents left you alone as a child, and you were afraid of every creak the wind wrenched out of your house. Or call to mind a time when you were lost in the woods and longed to hear the sound of a fellow hiker. Or the parties you attended without an escort. Or the evenings your spouse was gone, and you had no one to laugh with when you heard that good line on the TV sitcom or to sit with on a cold night in front of a cozy fire.

The truth is, divorce can feel like all those lonely moments happening to you at once. The myth is that ending the marriage is a guaranteed way to end your loneliness.

2. "You Can't Make Dead Coals Glow Again."

The truth of this myth is that few marriages can deliver the romantic feelings of courtship days forever. My wife and I also had to confront the fact that angry words and basic disagreements over several years had seriously damaged our capacity for romance. The blunt fact that "the feeling is gone" can be very real. The myth is that you can't recapture *some* feelings worth hanging onto. Actually, the determination to do just this can give you the unforeseen capacity for the rediscovery of romance.

As I said in chapter 9, separation and doing nothing saved us at this point. Again, I am not advocating separation as a blanket cure for a rocky marriage. I am just sharing our experience in which (a) absence really did make our hearts grow fonder; and (b) giving ourselves time to weigh the alternatives before rushing into divorce also gave romance the time it needed to slip up on us again.

Before you divorce because the feeling is gone, focus on *doing*, instead of *feeling*. As we've seen, doing loving things can allow loving feelings to follow, in time. Feelings have a way of clinging to your deeds while you're not looking. They will surprise you some morning when you look at your spouse, still asleep, and wonder how you could have been so angry at someone so loving.

3. "Adultery Would Be the End of My Marriage."
Chapter 4 showed that, as serious as adultery is, it occurs in the same "moral universe" as emotional blackmail, rejection, frigidity, and other lapses that often result in divorce. Even if a spouse has strayed out of sheer boredom, or because the opportunity was there, the marriage still might be salvageable.

The truth of adultery is that no breach of the marriage vows goes so deep and draws from an offended spouse such outrage. The myth is that genuine *repentance*—which must include both spouses turning around and going toward each other instead of away from each other—can't restore the trust that was once enjoyed.

If you are considering divorce because your spouse has been unfaithful, ask yourself if you can live with a penitent sinner. Remember that if you remarry, you'll be living with one, unless he or she is an angel—and unless you see one every time you look in a mirror.

4. "Split If Your Partner Can't Meet Your Needs."
Of course the truth of this myth is that we all have needs, and we all wish that the person to whom we're married could meet them. The myth comes in thinking that anyone can meet *all our needs.*

Here are some questions to ask if you're considering divorce because your needs aren't being met.

1. What needs are you talking about? (Actually list them, and let your spouse read them.)

2. Are they needs that have developed since you promised, "'Till death do us part"?

3. If so, have you given your spouse time to develop new capacities for understanding your new needs?

4. Did your spouse act attentive during courtship days, only to become insensitive and distant after marriage?

5. If so, have you changed in a way that may have contributed to your spouse's inattentiveness?

6. Wouldn't safe friendships and hobbies or activities outside the marriage be a less drastic way to deal with the problem than divorce?

When my wife and I were struggling in our marriage, she joined the singing group "Sweet Adelines." This not only fulfilled some of her needs that I could not meet; it also freed me from the cloying and oppressing feeling of having to meet all her needs. The new space this created actually drew us closer together. We were each healthier persons in our own right—less needy, slower to require of each other what neither could deliver. So we became more attractive to each other too.

5. "The Kids Would Be Better Off Not Seeing Us Fight—and Anyway, They Bounce Back Easily."
Please reread the evidence in chapter 3 that shows just how long, and how seriously, divorce can impact a child's life. Of course, they would be better off if you and your

spouse wouldn't fight—at least unfairly. That's the truth of this myth. But are you sure you have to divorce to bless your children with a more peaceful home?

If you divorce, they will still have to live in a world of conflict, angry words, even violence. How much better to teach them to deal with such realities in the context of a two-parent home. If you and your spouse will learn to negotiate, or to "fight *fair*," you could even equip your children with the negotiating skills and the realistic expectations necessary to make their own relationships work in the real world.

Conflict is not only a personal growth hormone. Viewed positively, it can be positively contagious: your kids could catch it in its most benevolent form.

As a last word, let me affirm the experiences of those who have dared, in these pages, to challenge the cultural assumption that divorce is the treatment of choice for an ailing marriage. Inevitable though divorce may be in some cases, these stories confirm the view that it is radical surgery, never to be taken lightly, and always to be preceded by a second opinion and a year—or two or three or four—of consideration.

As singles minister Gary Richmond says, "Fixing your marriage may be easier than breaking it. . . . If you give God an inch, He'll take a mile if you're willing to go along for the ride."[4]

ENDNOTES

Introduction
[1] *The Los Angeles Times,* 28 Nov. 1989.
[2] Diane Medved, *The Case Against Divorce* (New York: Donald I. Fine), p. 5.

Chapter 1
[1] In the *Waco* (Texas) *Tribune-Herald,* 26 Sept. 1986, p. 12A.
[2] David Lambert, "Coming Up Short," *Moody Monthly,* Oct. 1987, p. 16

Chapter 2
[1] Diane Medved, *The Case Against Divorce* (New York: Donald I. Fine, Inc., 1989), p. 227.
[2] Lenore Weitzman, *The Divorce Revolution* (New York: The Free Press, 1985), p. xii.
[3] Ibid., p. 323.
[4] "Study Links Divorce, Children's Illness," *The Arizona Daily Sun,* 13 Aug. 1990.
[5] Weitzman, p. xiv.
[6] Gary Richmond, "When Families Break Up: The Human Toll," *Focus on the Family* magazine, August 1989, p. 3.

⁷ Jim Talley, *Reconcilable Differences* (Nashville: Thomas Nelson Publishers, 1985), p. 26.
⁸ Deidre S. Laiken, *Daughters of Divorce* (New York: William Morrow and Company, 1981), p. 43.

Chapter 3
¹ Niki Scott, *Waco Tribune-Herald,* 12 Nov. 1986, p. 2C.
² *Daughters of Divorce,* p. 62.
³ Sonja Goldstein and Albert J. Solnit, *Divorce and Your Child* (New Haven: Yale University Press, 1984), p. 66.
⁴ "When Families Break Up: The Human Toll," *Focus on the Family* magazine, Aug. 1989, p. 4.
⁵ Niki Scott, *Waco Tribune Herald.*
⁶ Barbara Krantowitz, et al., "Breaking the Divorce Cycle," *Newsweek,* 13 Jan. 1992, p. 52.
⁷ Ibid., p. 53.
⁸ Linda Bird Francke, *Growing Up Divorced* (New York: Linden Press/Simon & Schuster, 1983).
⁹ *People* magazine in its issue of 29 May 1989.
¹⁰ From the Associated Press in the *Arizona Daily Sun,* 5 Aug. 1990.
¹¹ Judith S. Wallerstein and Sandra Blakeslee, *Second Chances: Men, Women & Children a Decade after Divorce* (New York City: Ticknor and Fields, 1989), pp. xvii-xviii.
¹² *Woman's Day,* 17 Jan. 1989.
¹³ Ibid.
¹⁴ Francke, loc. cit.
¹⁵ Ibid., p. 233.

Chapter 4
¹ It should be noted that this "exception clause" does not appear in the other Gospels—even in the parallel saying in Mark. Since Mark was, according to most scholars, the earliest Gospel to circulate among the early churches, many Christians no doubt lived under the more severe rule in Mark: marriage is for life—period. Then, as now, those whose lives did not meet this standard could only

fling themselves on the "mercy of the court" — Christ's limitless grace.

² See *Love Must Be Tough* (Waco, Texas: Word Publishing, 1983).

³ Joan Libman, "Therapists Begin Taking a Dim View of Divorce," *The Los Angeles Times*, 28 Nov. 1989.

⁴ Dalma Heyn, "When Divorce Is Not the Answer," *McCall's*, Aug. 1987, p. 29.

⁵ Ella Wheeler Wilcox, *Whatever Is, Is Best* (Boulder, Colo.: Blue Mountain Arts, Inc., 1975), pp. 62–63.

⁶ Annette Lawson, *Adultery* (New York: Basic Books, 1988), p. 296.

⁷ Ibid.

⁸ J. Allan Petersen, *The Myth of Greener Grass* (Wheaton, Ill.: Tyndale House Publishers, 1983), pp. 122–47.

Chapter 5

¹ Diane Medved, *The Case Against Divorce* (New York: Donald L. Fine, Inc., 1989), p. 20.

² Sharon Marshall, *Surviving Separation and Divorce* (Grand Rapids, Mich.: Baker Book House, 1988), p. 106.

³ John R.W. Stott, *Involvement: Social and Sexual Relationships in the Modern World* (Old Tappen, N.J.: Fleming H. Revell Co., 1985), p. 182.

Chapter 6

¹ Edmund Beagler, *Divorce Won't Help* (New York: Harper & Bros., 1948), p. 26.

² Augustus Y. Napier, with Carl A. Whitaker, *The Family Crucible* (New York: Bantam Books, 1978), p. 227. This is an excellent and lively description of how "family systems therapy" gets at the way family relationships, not just individual "problems," impacts family struggles.

³ "Computer Dating Leads Husband Back to Spouse," *Waco Tribune-Herald*, 15 Nov. 1986, p. 2A.

⁴ Dalma Heyn, "When Divorce Is Not the Answer," *McCall's*, Aug. 1987.

⁵ Joan Libman, "Therapists Begin Taking a Dim View of

Divorce," *The Los Angeles Times*, 28 Nov. 1989.

Chapter 7
[1] Mark Stuart and D'Esta Love, *Good News for Marriage* (Agoura Hills, Calif.: DMS Communications, 1987), p. 149.
[2] Bonnie and Frank's story is told by Jim Talley, in *Reconcilable Differences* (Nashville: Thomas Nelson, 1985).
[3] Ibid., p. 17.
[4] John Scanzoni, *Love and Negotiate* (Waco, Texas: Word Publishing, 1979).
[5] Ibid., p. 63.
[6] Gerald G. May, *Addiction and Grace* (San Francisco: Harper & Row, 1988), p. 167.
[7] David Viscott, *How to Live with Another Person* (New York: Pocket Books, 1983), pp. 19–20.
[8] Harold Straughn, *The Five Divorces of a Healthy Marriage* (St. Louis: CBP Press, 1986), p. 126.

Chapter 9
[1] "When Divorce Is Not the Answer," *McCall's*, August 1987, p. 28.
[2] Ibid., p. 30.
[3] "Death of a Marriage," *The Reader's Digest*, October 1987, p. 108.
[4] *Advice from a Failure* (New York: Stein and Day, 1976), p. 76.

Chapter 10
[1] Mircea Eliade, *The Myth of the Eternal Return* (Princeton, N.J.: Princeton University Press, 1954), p. 48.
[2] Harold Straughn, *The Five Divorces of a Healthy Marriage* (St. Louis: CBP Press, 1986), pp. 86–87.
[3] Annette Lawson, *Adultery* (New York: Basic Books, 1988), pp. 21–25. The author also shows that "The Myth of Me," or individualism, is another powerful factor in adultery, divorce, and remarriage.
[4] Gary Richmond, "When Families Break Up," *Focus on the Family* magazine, August 1989, p. 4.